TREASURES
FROM THE
EMBROIDERERS' GUILD
❖ COLLECTION ❖

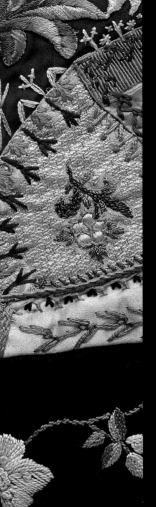

TREASURES
FROM THE
EMBROIDERERS' GUILD
❖ COLLECTION ❖

THE EMBROIDERERS' GUILD

Edited by Elizabeth Benn

A DAVID & CHARLES CRAFT BOOK

(*previous page*)

Patchwork cover, British *c*1880–1900.
Detail of a crazy patchwork cover pieced from plain and patterned dress and furnishing fabrics
EG 25 1988, 143cm (56½in) square. Given by Mrs Winifred Smith

(*below*)

Red silk-velvet slippers, probably Turkish, nineteenth century or later (see page 89)

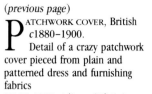
Photography by Julia Hedgecoe, unless otherwise credited

British Library Cataloguing in Publication Data
Treasures from the Embroiderers' Guild collection.
1. Embroidery, history
I. Benn, Elizabeth   II. Embroiderers' Guild
746.4409

ISBN 0-7153-9829-6

Typeset by Ace Filmsetting Ltd, Frome, Somerset and printed in Singapore by CS Graphics Pte Ltd for David & Charles plc
Brunel House   Newton Abbot   Devon

CONTENTS

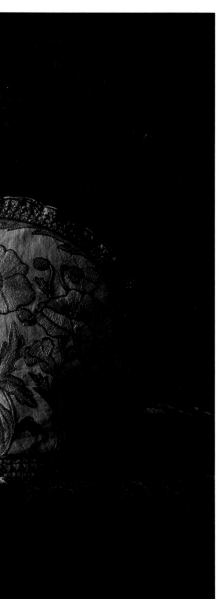

INTRODUCTION

Elizabeth Benn

T HE EMBROIDERERS' GUILD COLLECTION is unique in that it has in the main been donated by embroiderers to inspire and inform other embroiderers. It holds a very special place in the hearts of Guild members and other enthusiasts, as it has been assembled with great affection by those who care passionately about the subject.

When the Guild was founded in 1906, the vogue for studying old embroideries for inspiration was an ingrained part of the art needlework movement. It was natural therefore for the pioneering members of the Guild to accumulate fragments of old British and foreign embroideries which could be circulated among members in portfolios – quaintly named 'model boxes'.

Members were continually being urged to find embroideries for these portfolios and under the royal patronage of Queen Mary during the 1920s and 1930s the Guild was given many pieces such as quilts, costumes and hangings that were too large to circulate. These donations formed the nucleus of the present Collection, and Queen Mary, an enthusiastic embroiderer and the Patron from 1924 to 1953, donated a dozen important pieces, several of which are illustrated in this book. The Collection has grown dramatically since those days and now contains about ten thousand examples of embroidery, and lace, from many cultures. In 1989 the Collection was given museum status by the Museums and Galleries Commission.

To an embroiderer, a fragment covered with stitchery can be every bit as fascinating as a complete article. The minute detail of each stitch is of paramount importance: what type of stitch, where it comes from, which family it belongs to, how it is done and what threads are used. Today there are plenty of books illustrating every possible type of stitch so there is no need to repeat William Morris's exercise in unpicking old embroideries in order to learn how the stitches were done. Each country has a repertoire of stitches and these variations can be seen in the chapters of this book.

Different aspects of the Collection have been the subject of many articles, particularly in *Embroidery*, the Guild's quarterly magazine, but also in several

T HREE TEACOSIES spanning nearly a century from the Victorian era, with a tablecloth from 1890.
In the centre is a Berlinwork design in tent stitch with grisaille beads, 1860. Right, an art needlework style design in silk on linen by Elsie Marianne Grimes, 1910–20. Left, a sketchy design by Frances Beal, machine embroidered in silk on organdie by Dorothy Benson, 1946. The tablecloth has an Anglo-Indian border
EG 5883, 28 × 44cm (11 × 17¼in). EG 154 1983, 24 × 34cm (9½ × 13¼in). EG 1035, 26 × 33cm (10¼ × 13in). EG 80 1982, 77cm (30¼in)

exhibition catalogues, notably *Three Hundred Years of Embroidery*. This book, however, is the first comprehensive publication.

To enjoy old embroideries to the full, it helps to have the mind of a detective. Traditional patterns are often copied slavishly by successive generations. Also, embroiderers have always had a tendency to follow rather than lead fashion which makes dating a piece extremely difficult. Then there is the almost impossible question of whether the embroidery is the work of a professional or an amateur.

We are fortunate that a great deal of research has been carried out on old textiles during this century. For instance, the original printed sources of many of the early English embroidery patterns have been located. At a more humble level many of us would like to learn the origins of embroideries brought back from abroad, perhaps by relations. Are they the genuine ethnic article, or something made for the tourists? The answer might be in the European or Indian chapters (Chapters 5 and 4).

Take the humble bath towel. How many of us realise it began life as an exquisitely embroidered cloth to be 'shown off' in the local baths in Turkey? For generations Turkish towels have been popular buys with travellers, but can you tell the difference between a towel, a turban cover and a sash?

A glance at the Index will show that silk has always been the preferred thread. The fascinating history and origins of this always expensive thread can be found in Chapter 6, and it is interesting to discover how in some cultures it is used quite economically – as a surface darned stitch, using as little thread as possible on the unseen fabric back.

The cross-fertilisation of patterns from one country to another, which has existed since trade between countries began, can be followed through the illustrations. For instance, the oriental pagodas, bridges and stylised trees which arrived in Britain at the end of the seventeenth century from China sometimes came in the form of embroidered cloth from India.

Today the influences of other cultures are more likely to be seen through the eyes of the artists, who interpreted them in their own work. Embroidery is now firmly established as an art form though it has taken almost a century for this to be achieved. It was the art needlework movement, and in particular the teachers at the Glasgow School of Art, who persuaded embroiderers to make their own designs rather than rely upon pattern drawers and printed sources. The number of creative embroiderers, of all abilities, has increased enormously in the past twenty years and for them the range of modern materials, threads and dyes is very much more extensive than it was twenty years ago, as is access to sources of inspiring material through travel and illustrated books.

The Guild owns what is possibly one of the most important groups of twentieth-century embroideries by artist-craftspeople assembled in any one place. These are just the latest additions to a comprehensive collection of British embroideries, dating from the seventeenth century to the present day, which provide an excellent survey of decorative textiles.

The Collection has been in the care of a professional curator for only the past ten years and, before 1981, when the Guild was granted a grace and favour apartment in Hampton Court Palace, the conditions under which such precious embroideries were stored were distinctly unsatisfactory. The headquarters moved several times in central London, and the laundry baskets and cardboard boxes containing the collection were piled high on metal racks in these various, rather cramped, premises. During World War II they were even dispersed among the membership in the country to keep them safe from possible bomb damage.

The splendid new headquarters in Hampton Court Palace at last provided the Guild with sufficient space to store the embroideries in specially designed cabinets fitted with lightweight plastic trays. The Collection continues to grow through donations and acquisitions, which fill gaps in the historic sequence and keep abreast of new developments in the craft.

The first major exhibition of the Collection, 'One Thousand Years of Embroidery', held at Celanese House in central London in 1971 by courtesy of Courtaulds, was followed by other smaller exhibitions in Britain. By the mid-1980s a series of touring exhibitions, each with a theme, was sent to museums and art galleries around the British Isles, and to Australia and Japan.

The themes have included Indian embroideries, whitework, plants and flowers, 'The Needle's Eye' tracing the development of embroidery as an art form, and '300 Years of Embroidery' with the best of the early British embroideries. The travelling exhibitions give the Guild members, now numbering around 11,000 in 150 branches throughout the British Isles, the opportunity to appreciate 'their' Collection without having to travel to Hampton Court Palace.

The original intention that this 'study' Collection should be accessible to the membership holds good today, though in a modified form. It is now divided into three groups: the main Collection, the handling Collection, and the portfolios, now called 'study folios', which have been changed to keep pace with the requirements of the modern embroiderer. The packages, which may uniquely be hired for a modest fee by members, are just as likely to contain instructions for making felt or paper, as examples of historic embroidery.

The exhibition room in the Guild's headquarters always has a selection of embroideries on view. They are accompanied by a set of study boards designed to encourage visitors to take a closer look at the objects and really digest what they are seeing. This scheme is backed up by lectures from the Curator, and practical sessions with the Embroidery Adviser.

The Collection has received magnificent donations in the past and, even now, when antique textiles are becoming scarce and extremely valuable, members continue to give pieces which they could sell for many thousands of pounds, pieces they have treasured themselves and which they do not want to be buried in a store room as happens to bequests to so many museums. They know that pieces given to the Collection will be fully and properly appreciated by other embroidery enthusiasts from all over the world.

CHAPTER 1

FROM TUDOR COIFS TO THE TWENTIETH CENTURY

British Embroideries

Lynn Szygenda

BRITISH EMBROIDERIES, gathered largely from donors, form the largest part of the Embroiderers' Guild Collection. They span four centuries; the earliest were embroidered during the last years of Elizabeth's reign (*d*1603), and the most modern pieces were worked within months of the writing of this book. During these past four centuries embroidery in Britain has developed into a major domestic art: many of the embroidered furnishings and costume pieces in the British collection were worked by women in the home. Created out of necessity or for pleasure, these pieces illustrate the changing popular tastes in design and embroidery technique. The Collection also houses examples of professional embroidery in the sumptuous costume pieces of the seventeenth and eighteenth centuries; and the skills employed in commercially produced whitework pieces are evident in the late-eighteenth-century embroidered muslin aprons and nineteenth-century Ayrshirework. Since the 1930s, embroiderers have taken an increasingly experimental approach to their work. The Guild's Collection of contemporary British embroidery provides a vibrant record of the art today, revealing it as innovative and vital. Illustrated here are some of the most important British embroideries in the Collection.

(*opposite*)
PATCHWORK BEDCOVER, English, late nineteenth century.
A patchwork of woven silks, and pieced in 'tumbling blocks' design to create an illusion of three dimensions. It is boarded with a strip of crimson-plush-coloured cotton sateen
EG 2549, 188 × 204cm (6ft 1¼in × 6ft 7½in). Given by Mrs G. Foxton and Mrs M. Hodge

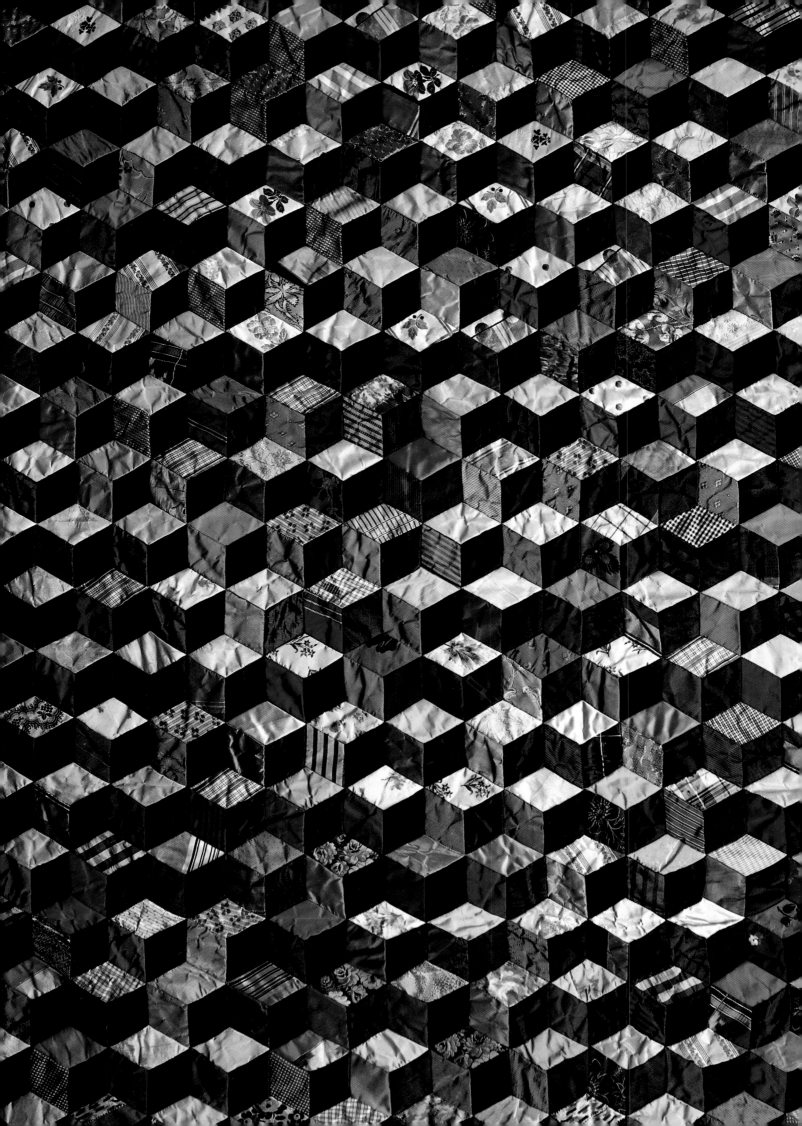

SEVENTEENTH-CENTURY COSTUMES AND HANGINGS

The decades which linked the Tudor and Stuart dynasties in the early seventeenth century formed one of the most exuberant periods in the history of embroidery. Domestic embroidery particularly flourished and blossomed, and the makers, nameless numbers of amateur embroideresses, have since become renowned for their skill and enthusiasm. Indeed the surviving examples of their work display such a high level of expertise that many historians have shrunk from describing this embroidery as amateur, and prefer the term domestic work which reflects both the general basis of production and the application of the embroidery.

The earliest British embroideries which the Guild owns date from the closing and opening years of the sixteenth and seventeenth centuries. Most of these pieces are items of informal headwear and they are some of the most charming embroideries in the Collection. They include five coif panels stitched *c*1600, which beautifully illustrate the prowess of their makers and the popular designs of the day. Coifs were close-fitting day bonnets worn by fashionable women in the home, perhaps for receiving visitors. The Collection also contains a man's nightcap of the same date which was not intended for sleeping in but is better regarded as the male equivalent of the coif. It seems that coifs were sometimes accompanied by matching triangular forehead cloths supposedly worn to prevent wrinkles, but which were surely more useful in covering up already existing lines.

Despite being regarded as informal costume, surviving coifs are invariably richly embroidered in the finest materials. Some coifs have been embroidered in monochrome threads, black and red being particular favourites. Two of the Guild's coifs use white linen threads on a white linen ground to create patterns either in cutwork with needlelace fillings, or rich surface stitchery enhanced by a sprinkling of metal spangles. Much more sumptuous coifs have been embroidered in polychrome silks and metal threads with applied seed pearls as well as spangles. Three of the Guild's coif panels are exquisite examples of this combined use of coloured silks and metal threads. Their coiling plant designs are worked on grounds of fine linen in stitches which bring a raised element to the work, presaging the three-dimensional embroidery popular in the mid-seventeenth century.

Many coifs, including those on pages 14/15 (EG 16 and 79 1982), used metal threads in plaited braid or chain stitches to work the stems, and a variety of detached buttonhole

stitches to create fruit and flower motifs in relief. Today many people are captivated by the informality of such designs which mix flowers and fruit in seemingly incongruous combinations: the grape with the pea plant; a formal lily with a humble pansy. To us a strange choice perhaps, but one which reflects the former importance and status of different plants. It has been suggested that the coiling stem is a descendant from Celtic design, most famously interpreted in *Opus Anglicanum* as the 'tree of Jesse'. It seems plausible that after the Reformation of the Church, professional embroiderers formerly providing ecclesiastical commissions should apply their designs, such as the fruiting vine, to secular uses. Similarly the appropriation of church vestments for domestic use may have helped to widen the popularity of formerly religious motifs.

Richly worked embroidery designs were not confined to accessories: wonderfully lively patterns of flowers, birds, bees, butterflies and caterpillars crept and fluttered over a range of garments. This output was probably shared between amateur and professional embroiderers, but the splendid outfits required for state pageant, civic ceremony and formal occasions generally were entirely created by professional hands.

Amongst the Guild's Collection of seventeenth-century embroideries is a pair of gloves (EG 1) page 14, worked *c*1600–25, which are a fine example of professional workmanship. At this time gloves retained symbolic associations, and could be used to seal a contract, offer a challenge or be given as a favour as well as worn for practical purposes (see *Gloves* by Valerie Cumming). Highly decorated gloves cut from perfumed leather and embellished with embroidery, lace, seed pearls and spangles were given as gifts amongst the wealthy, or to visiting dignitaries. The heavy ornamentation and impractical cut of the hand parts limited or prevented the glove from having any practical use. The finger length of such gloves is often noticeably longer, and perhaps more slender than those of the average hand. Valerie Cumming has suggested that this extended cut was a fashionable trend followed by people who wished to emulate the appearance of Queen Elizabeth's long narrow fingers. Because men and women of fashion were equally lavish in their dress it is difficult to decide the sex of the original owners, but Cumming sensibly attributes shorter, narrower gloves to a woman's use.

At the outset of the seventeenth century an array of

textile furnishings was required to create warmth, comfort and ornament. Cold walls required hangings; beds needed furnishings and linen; and hard wooden stools and seats wanted padded cushions to make them comfortable. Professional and amateur embroiderers collaborated to varying degrees to satisfy a household's textile needs. The noted skill of amateur embroideresses, coupled with the availability of ready-made designs, means that the origin of much early-Stuart embroidery is difficult to determine. Professional involvement can be gauged by looking at several factors: the scale of the work, the complexity of the design and level of draughtsmanship, and the uniformly high quality of technique used.

Amongst the Guild's seventeenth-century embroideries is a small panel (EG 3819) perhaps intended for a cushion cover, which is almost certainly the work of an amateur. As the illustration reveals, the design is composed of an assortment of plant and flower, animal and insect motifs which are very similar to those found in early-seventeenth-century pattern books. Pattern books for various crafts had been printed since the early sixteenth century; as the decades passed these were plundered and supplemented by subsequent publishers so that by the Stuart period a variety of printed patterns were available to the amateur embroideress. Illustrated Bibles and volumes of classical literature, herbals and bestiaries were also popularly resorted to by embroidery designers. Motifs from the printed page could be copied or pricked and pounced on to the embroidery ground fabric. The simplicity of the latter method may have enthused the designer of this panel to cram in as many motifs as possible. These stiff stitch outlined sprigs recall the many plant motifs copied from botanical woodcuts in the illustrated herbals. Intended as a complete record such illustrations often depicted the root, stem, bud, flower, leaf and fruit simultaneously on one plant. Several of these elements have been retained in the seventeeth-century embroidered versions.

Where a lightweight ground fabric was used the embroidery could be worked directly on to it, but when a heavier fabric was needed an appliqué method of decorating was more suitable. Often motifs were worked on a canvas ground in tent stitch, then cut out and applied to the heavier furnishing. The motifs were known as slips – an appropriate word given its horticultural associations and the popularity of plant motifs. The thistle slip illustrated (EG 4485), page 16, is one of three in the Collection which once decorated the same velvet ground – each slip is still attached to a remnant of this fabric. The slips use silk threads embroidered in tent stitch on a canvas ground and are edged with couched metal thread. Not only does this edging echo the heavy outline of a

E NGLISH SAMPLER, late seventeenth century, and Italian border, late sixteenth century, showing similar designs. The linen sampler, English 1690s, embroidered with silk and linen threads shows similar designs to that used in the late-sixteenth-/ early-seventeenth-century Italian border of linen *burato* embroidered with silk threads in back stitch, perhaps a century earlier
EG 3881, 68.5 × 19cm (2ft 2¾in × 7½in). EG 5380, 6.5 × 24cm (2½ × 9½in)

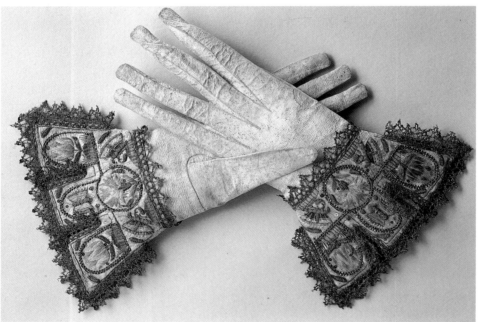

(*above*)

COIF, ENGLISH, early seventeenth century. Linen ground fabric embroidered with silk and silver-gilt threads, silver strips and a few spangles. The stems are worked in plaited chain, whilst the flowers are embroidered in detached lacework. The coif has been opened out to show the complete embroidery design
EG 16, 25.5 × 43cm (10in × 1ft 4¾in). Given by Lady Mary Cayley

PAIR OF GLOVES, English, c1600–25. Kid or doeskin gloves with tabbed gauntlets, constructed from two layers of linen overlaid by embroidered silk and trimmed with silver-gilt lace. The embroidery uses floss silk and silver-gilt thread, silver strip, metal purl and spangles
EG 1, length 32cm (12½in). Given by Lady Mary Vaughn and Lady Reigate

(*right*)

FLORAL PANEL, possibly a cushion cover, English, mid-seventeenth century. Linen embroidered with silk threads. The rococo stitched motifs and hillocks are outlined with back stitch on a brick stitched ground. The floral sprigs, rabbit and insects were probably from contemporary printed sources such as *The Needle's Excellency* published in 1634 by James Boler
EG 3819, 22 × 35.5cm (8½in × 1ft 2in) (Photograph: Dudley Moss)

(*above*)

Panel, possibly from a coif, English, early seventeenth century.
Linen embroidered with a scrolling pattern in silver-gilt thread, the flowers, animals and birds in varied techniques including plaited braid, chain and detached needlelace stitches in silk with metal strip and spangles. The embroidery is highly textural, the top layer of the peapod peels back to reveal golden peas, and some of the flowers are worked over padding whilst others, and the bees' wings, are detached
EG 79 1982, 22.5 × 42.5cm (8¾in × 1ft 4½in). Given by the NDS

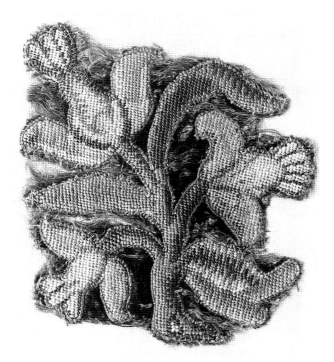

A THISTLE 'SLIP' applied to velvet, first half of the seventeenth century. Canvas embroidered with floss silks in tent stitch, the outline emphasised by couched metal thread. The motif was probably copied from a printed pattern book or herbal
EG 4485. 13 × 11.5cm (5 × 4½in)

B LACKWORK MOTIF, English, sixteenth century. Linen embroidered with silk and silver-gilt threads in double running (blackwork) and chain stitches (outline). These two floral sprigs may have been taken from a supporting strapwork of blackwork embroidery, also in the Collection, that was probably used for a long cushion. The blackwork has suffered due to the effects of the mordant holding the black dye which eventually rots the silk
EG 207. 8 × 8cm (3 × 3in)

woodcut image, it served the practical purpose of binding and disguising the cut canvas edge.

The blackwork honeysuckle motif illustrated (EG 207) is more formal. The highly stylised motif is decorated with stitches in a variety of geometric filling patterns. Such formality would have been more popular in the sixteenth, rather than seventeenth century. It is one of three pieces of blackwork dating from the late 1590s which are the earliest embroideries in the British section of the Collection. The honeysuckle is partnered by a carnation and fragments of linen bands. In 1936 John Nevinson speculated that the bands were part of a design of strapwork medallions which encased the flowers, and that the original embroidered object may have been a long pillow cover from which the motifs were cut during the seventeenth century to be reapplied in a more modern style.

Monochrome embroidery contrasted effectively with a white ground fabric, and it continued in popularity into the seventeenth century. However, the designs became more naturalistic.

The large red crewel wool embroidered panel illustrated (EG 731), which may have been an altar frontal, is an unusual furnishing textile stitched *c*1650. The materials and techniques are typical of the mid-century years, usually associated with bird and animal motifs or the large branching plants which provide the intermediary stage between the tightly coiled coif patterns and the later Stuart 'tree of life' (see below). This panel illustrates a series of Old and New Testament stories. The embroidery stitches and monochrome wools used seem to emulate the appearance of woodcuts, from which the designs may have been derived. In 1585 in Antwerp Gerard de Jode published a set of engravings depicting biblical stories, which he had taken from drawings by Martin de Vos. The collection proved popular with embroidery designers: Pauline Johnstone has pointed out that the red crewel nativity scene and Hagar appear to be derived from de Jode's engravings. Several images in this hanging appear in other embroideries of the period indicating a common, popular design source.

The large hanging illustrated (EG 1282), embroidered with a coiling tree, probably formed part of a set of bedcurtains. It was worked *c*1700, and is a beautiful example of the most highly skilled professional work. Sinuous tree forms were frequently embroidered by amateurs in the later seventeenth century, but their designs were rarely so complex, or their stitches so richly varied as those used on this panel. A range of stitches have been employed to create a highly textured surface pattern in crewel wools (which have retained their original rich colours).

Anyone making a survey of seventeenth-century embroideries will be familiar with several of the motifs used in this hanging: there seems to have been a core of popular images recorded in pattern books, engravings and model embroideries which were used repeatedly. The development of the 'tree of life', as this design is often known, was heavily influenced by a vogue for oriental design which grew during the seventeenth century. Throughout the early decades of this century a limited number of Chinese artefacts were imported to Europe: enough to create a cult, but not enough to satisfy a growing demand. Consequently, European designers and craftsmen began producing their own work in imitation of Chinese pieces. In the mid-seventeenth century Indian dyed and painted cotton goods were exported to England but the designs were not popular, so the English merchants required the Indian craftsmen to follow designs more suited to European tastes. The designs sent out from England to India probably included European versions of Chinese tree designs, and perhaps other motifs such as Chinese exotic birds. Confusion over the geography of the world filled European minds. China and India were massed together as the far-flung mysterious East, and Europeans believed that either land could create the 'oriental' designs they desired.

Inevitably, as they worked, Indian craftsmen altered the European chinoiserie designs to reflect their own artistic traditions. The dyed and painted cottons they created were hugely popular in Europe where they inspired many embroidery designs. Perhaps this explains the mixture of European and oriental-type motifs combined in one design – for example Britain's native squirrel perched near a highly exotic plumed bird, a tree bearing oakleaves springing from hillocks reminiscent of Chinese

rock formations. In the hanging shown here, the Chinese asymmetrical tree has surrendered to a coiling stem more in keeping with the European baroque style.

A feature of the Commonwealth and later Stuart periods is the group of embroideries worked by girls in order to exhibit their prowess in needlework. The Guild owns two panels cut from different spot samplers (not illustrated) stitched early in the seventeenth century as reference works of stitches and designs. The motifs are arranged randomly, reflecting the way in which the embroiderer recorded useful techniques and motifs as she encountered them. Such arrangements contrast with the neat patterns seen on later seventeenth-century samplers. Many survive from this period, and were stitched largely as a technique exercise. Indeed the banded patterns decorating the narrow strips of linen such as that illustrated (EG 3881), page 13, were well out of style when they were stitched in the mid-seventeenth and late seventeenth century. Printed books and commercially drawn patterns were more likely to be consulted than samplers by embroiderers at this time. Many of the Guild's seventeenth-century band samplers carry stitched alphabets and numerals suggesting a growing conventional educational use of embroidery. Today many adult

Needlelace cuff, English, c1630.
Fine linen detachable cuff decorated with scallops of needlelace. The technique of building up stitched motifs on a gridwork of threads gave a geometric appearance. Here, however, the fine scallops at the edge are used to create a more fluid design
EG 166, overall depth 20cm (7¾in). Given by Lady Lawrence (Photograph: Dudley Moss)

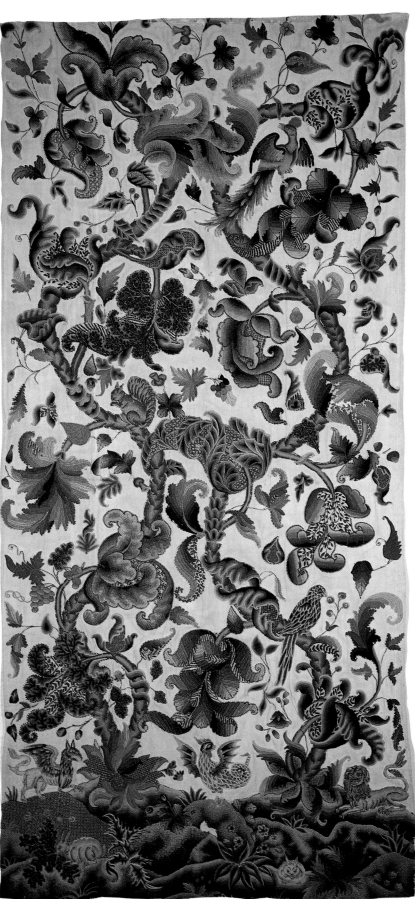

(*left*)
CREWELWORK HANGING
showing a magnificent blend
of Eastern and Western
design influences, probably from a
bed set, English *c*1700.
The twisting oriental-style trees
with large leaves are filled with a
variety of animals ranging from an
English squirrel and rabbit to the
more exotic lion and phoenix. The
linen twill ground is embroidered
with crewel wools in an extensive
range of stitches. It has been
remounted in recent decades. The
skilled drawing of the design and
the excellent embroidery clearly
reveal the piece as professional
work, but it is also a design which
would have been popularly
attempted by amateurs
EG 1282, 242 × 110cm
(7ft 10½in × 3ft 7in). Given by
Mrs St Osyth Wood (Photograph:
Dudley Moss)

(*right*)
A RAISED WORK CASKET (lid
illustrated) with scenes of
David and Bathsheba,
English, *c*1650–75.
The cream-coloured satin is
embroidered in raisedwork
techniques (popularly known as
stumpwork) in silk and chenille
threads, coiled metal wire painted
or covered with coloured thread.
Panels of mica are used for
windows, glass beads for eyes for
a fish and stag, and the king, dog
and maidservant wear tiny
seedpearl ornaments. Detached
lace stitchery is extensively used
for three-dimensional fruit,
flowers, tentflap and clothing and
over padding to form some of the
birds, beasts and architectural
features. The figures have slender,
carved wooden hands, embroidery
over padding and carved wooden
shapes. The illustration is
professionally drawn from an
engraving in *Thesaurus Veteris*
Testamenti by Gerard de Jode,
Antwerp, 1585
EG 48 1987, 28 × 39 × 14cm
(11 × 15¼ × 5½in). Given
by Miss Hester Clough

(*above*)

CREWELWORK HANGING depicting biblical stories, possibly an altar frontal, English *c*1650s.

The central figures are Adam and Eve in the Garden of Eden. The other biblical scenes, from the top right going clockwise, show the adoration of the shepherds, the

finding of Moses, the expulsion of Hagar, and the adoration of the Kings. The linen and cotton twill fabric is embroidered in red crewel wool in stem, brick, back,

speckling, detached and herringbone stitches
EG 731, 78 × 145.5cm (2ft 6½in × 4ft 8¾in). Given by the NDS

TWO SAMPLERS showing 'boxers', linen embroidered with silk threads, English, mid-seventeenth century. Each sampler has the characteristically long, narrow format of the period. The horizontally arranged patterns were derived from fashions of earlier decades, perhaps dating back to the sixteenth century when floral bands were used to decorate borders, collars and cuffs. The wider sampler shows an unusual combination of figures, animals and birds which originated in printed form. Each sampler has a figure known as 'the boxer' because of the sideways pugilistic stance. In the wider sampler the boxer appears clothed and in the lower is naked; in both cases they carry an object in their hands
EG 23 1987, 91 × 25cm (2ft 11½in × 9¾in). EG 29 1987, 75 × 21cm (29½ × 8¼ in). Given by Miss Hester Clough

SAMPLER (detail), English, late seventeenth century. This decorative strip from a linen sampler embroidered with linen thread shows the skill of contemporary embroiderers. The iris and rose motifs are worked in detached buttonhole stitch built up on a framework of laid threads *EG 7 1982. complete size 49.5 × 16.5cm (1ft 7¼in × 6½in)*

provided fashionable costume accessories and trimmings during the seventeenth century, an example being the linen cuff edging illustrated (EG 166, page 17) with a needlelace border.

From about the middle of the century, changes in interior design gradually brought about the discarding of textile hangings in favour of wooden panelling, and, in costume, plain silks became more fashionable than embroidered fabrics. Ironically as the need for embroidered decoration diminished, needlework skills increased in importance as a desirable female accomplishment. Embroidered pictures, mirror frames, baskets and caskets became popular alternative vehicles for displaying female talent. Techniques varied but scenes and motifs recurred with regularity, being derived from a range of 'mass-produced' commercially available patterns. The tent-stitched picture (EG 5860) and the casket workbox (EG 48 1987) decorated with raised work, both illustrated, use several similar motifs, made to look different through the techniques used. The tiny tent stitches which work the pictorial panel often excite the amazement of visitors, who then go on to marvel at the diligence and imagination which was expended in decorating the casket. The raised effects which are a feature of the box's embroidered panel have been achieved in several ways. A great deal of detached buttonholing has been used to create structures which are applied to the ground fabric, sometimes over padding or wooden moulded shapes. Sections of woven fabric have also been embroidered, cut and applied to simulate costume. Bulky coils of metal wire, and lengths of chenille thread were couched to create the foliage of trees or the texture of grass. Amazingly these virtuoso pieces were sometimes tackled by girls as young as twelve years old – as the culmination of their needlework education.

embroiderers are daunted by the level of expertise exhibited in band samplers signed and dated as the work of a child. It is comforting to speculate on how many trial samplers may have been dejectedly abandoned before the poor child produced a piece worthy of preservation.

Band samplers demonstrate a range of stitches and often include examples of whitework embroidery. The detail illustrated (EG 7 1982) is a sampler worked entirely in whitework techniques, the flowers being worked in needlelace. Needle-stitched and bobbin-woven laces

PANEL, the finding of Moses amongst the bulrushes, English mid-seventeenth century.
Linen embroidered with tent stitch in silk threads. The work is unfinished – the faces have not been stitched. The central scene is surrounded by a selection of unrelated, popular plant and animal motifs. The layout of the panel, which largely disregards perspective and scale, and the choice of incidental motifs, is similar to that used in the red crewelwork panel and the raised workbox (pages 19 and 18)
EG 5860, 24.5 × 34cm (9½in × 1ft 1¼in). Given by the NDS

POCKET BOOK, English, mid-eighteenth century.
Silk fabric embroidered with silk threads in long and short stitches to create a naturalistic effect. This type of design would also appear on costume and illustrates the move away from the stiffer sprigs seen earlier in the century
EG 2516, 39.5 × 10cm (1ft 3½in × 4in). Given by Mrs Newberry

Pictorial embroideries,
English, 1790–1800.
The silk ground fabrics are
embroidered with silk threads and
have some painted areas. Most of
the coloured embroidery is carried
out in long and short stitches to
create a realistic effect. The
printwork elephant is in straight
stitches to re-create the
appearance of an engraving or
etching. The man with the horn is
reminiscent of a similar figure in
an engraving by Bartolozzi after a
painting by Angelica Kauffmann.
The oval picture represents a
muse, and illustrates the late-
eighteenth-century classical taste
*Elephant: EG 237 1983, 11.5 ×
14cm (4½ × 5½in). Muse: EG 233
1983, 26 × 21cm (10 × 8in).
Pastoral pair: EG 235 1983, 20.5
× 16cm (8 × 6¼in). Bequest of
Miss C. M. Irons*

EIGHTEENTH-CENTURY ACCESSORIES AND SAMPLERS

During the eighteenth century, embroidery became confirmed as a fashionable leisure pursuit for ladies. A range of delightful, often personal embroidered items survive in the Guild Collection as a record of a popular eighteenth-century pastime. Amongst these are two pocket books; one signed MC and dated 1749, and a second later piece (EG 2516, illustrated) embroidered in the mid-eighteenth century. Cases such as these were used as general holdalls, perhaps for letters. As well as dividing pockets, the earlier case has three layered squares of felted fabric used for holding pins and needles, or perhaps as pen wipers, and it is decorated throughout with canvaswork embroidery. The technique brings a rather rigid stylised appearance to the motifs which contrasts markedly with the more naturalistic flower sprays embroidered on the later pocket book. Here surface stitchery on a closely woven satin ground has allowed a much more realistic interpretation of the design. This is noticeable in much of the later-eighteenth-century embroidery.

Pockets were a much more intimate method of storing and carrying useful items. Women wore pear-shaped pockets, singly or in pairs secured to a waistband and hidden beneath the petticoats. The bulky shape assumed by filled pockets would have been well disguised by layers of dress. Despite being hidden, pockets were frequently embroidered. The two early- to mid-century pocket tops in the Collection (not illustrated) have been prettily embroidered with floral sprays in silk threads, either for personal use or as presents.

Amongst the Guild's eighteenth-century pictorial embroideries is a set of silkwork pictures (EG 237 1983, 233 1983, 235 1983, 3917). Towards the close of the century, embroidering such items became a popular pursuit for accomplished ladies. This type of work takes its name from the use of silk or satin ground fabrics, since the embroidery itself was carried out in silk, chenille and sometimes woollen yarns. The background elements of a design were painted on to the silk fabric as were the faces and limbs of foreground figures. Silkwork was the perfect vehicle for displaying two desirable female talents: painting and embroidering. A surviving nineteenth-century American advertisement indicates that unscrupulous ladies could engage professionals to provide the paintwork, so disguising their own deficiencies. Indeed the quality of the painting sometimes exceeds that of the embroidery, suggesting either an imbalance of talents or another, more expert hand at work. In some surviving examples, coloured and cut paper faces and limbs have been applied to the silk grounds.

Engravings after popular paintings provided many silkwork designs. Rustic settings for romantic and sentimental scenes predominated. A taste for classical antiquity was reflected in the number of embroideries which illustrated neo-classically draped figures. Often these were posed mourning a lost literary author or hero: Shakespeare, Werther and Goethe were particularly lamented.

Illustrated with the silkwork pictures is a form of embroidery which is known as printwork because the stitchery attempts to re-create the appearance of etchings and engravings. Embroiderers used monochrome threads in long straight stitches to achieve this aim. Pauline Johnstone has suggested that the elephant shown here may be adapted from an illustration in Thomas Bewick's *A General History of Quadrupeds*, 1790. The turbanned head has been stitched in two shades of brown silk thread which have at times been mistaken for human hair. In fact, embroideries using hair are rare.

Sampler making maintained its popularity throughout the eighteenth century. Gradually the long narrow bands of linen which formed the basis of seventeenth-century samplers were replaced by square or rectangular ground fabrics cut from longer pieces of cloth. Avril Colby has suggested that this development arose from the decreasing need to economise with material supplies, but it is perhaps more obviously an indication of the growing use of samplers as decorative, often pictorial pieces. The later-eighteenth-century pictorial sampler illustrated (EG 2091) shows composition typical of the period, with motifs arranged round a central image, or verse, and the whole enclosed within an embroidered border. It is interesting to see how the 'new' samplers continued to use patterns and motifs taken from earlier embroideries. This sampler contains the stylised floral wave patterns frequently seen in seventeenth-century band samplers, and the diamond shapes stitched into the lower corners are reminiscent of geometric motifs recorded in early-seventeenth-century spot samplers. This habit of borrowing has continued in twentieth-century sampler making. Now it is traditional to create sampler designs inspired by seventeenth-, eighteenth- and nineteenth-century models.

The frequent appearance of stitched alphabets and numerals has encouraged a popular belief that sampler making was an educational exercise. A feature of many

EMBROIDERED SILK 'printwork' picture, English, 1796.
The cream silk ground is embroidered with brown and black silk threads. The head is taken from an etching by Robert Blyth after a pen and ink drawing by John Hamilton Mortimer. Inscribed on the reverse is 'Worked by Eliza Skinner 1796'
EG 3917, diameter 23cm (9in)

eighteenth-century samplers is the inclusion of lines taken from hymns, psalms and Bible passages. One sampler (not illustrated) in the Collection carries the Lord's Prayer and the Creed, both precisely worked in minute cross stitch. It is signed 'Mary Lucas workt this in the twelvt year of her age May 6 1726'. As the century progressed, stitched pious verse increased in popularity, perhaps as a means of inculcating filial obedience, diligence and the basics of Christian morality. *Divine and Moral Songs for Children* published in 1720 became a source of sampler verse. The author, Dr Isaac Watts, believed that moral precepts could be most firmly remembered in verse form. For many children the labour of stitching surely made the verse unforgettable.

Towards the end of the century a fashion developed for stitching map samplers. In many of these the decorative elements vie strongly with the educational content. The Guild owns such a sampler which is entitled 'A Map of England and Wales'. The counties and countries have been outlined in couched coloured silks and the county names crammed in in cross stitch. The map is enclosed within an ornately embroidered floral border. Panels such as this were particularly popular, whilst more adventurous geographers created three-dimensional globe

samplers. In some examples the inaccurately drawn maps indicate the work of young pupils, but from the 1780s printed outlines of counties, countries and continents could be purchased for oversewing (see *Samplers* by Avril Colby).

Many eighteenth-century samplers which demonstrated a valuable practical skill were dominated by their decorative appeal. The 'AT' who stitched the technically excellent darning sampler illustrated (EG 14 1990) may have been a young girl with considerable talent, or a tutor demonstrating her skills. Darning samplers appear to have been popular during the turn of the eighteenth and nineteenth centuries. Holes were cut into the even-weave ground fabric and meticulously mended with coloured embroidery silks in a variety of patterned darns. In this sampler the decorative effect has been enhanced by stitching the darns in ornamental shapes to create pleasing motifs.

Eighteenth-century embroiderers did not devote their energies exclusively to embroidering small ornamental and personal items. In the earlier decades, wealthy women in particular persisted in displaying their talents through the production of extensive suites of embroidered furnishings and small pictures such as the one

Ictorial sampler, English, late eighteenth century. Fine woollen canvas embroidered with silk threads in cross, tent, rice and rococo stitches. The sampler shows the pictorial emphasis which had evolved by this date; it also incorporates earlier patterns which show the tenacity of designs given a traditional application, such as stylised band patterns, strawberry slips and the two geometric diamonds in the bottom corners *EG 2091, 41 × 32cm (1ft 4in × 1ft ½in). Given by Miss Henwood (Photograph: Dudley Moss)*

D ARNING SAMPLER, English, late eighteenth century. Very fine linen ground embroidered with silk threads, mostly in pattern darning with outlining in stem and buttonhole edging. The various panel sections are divided by pulledwork *EG 14 1990. 34 × 33cm (1ft 1¼in × 1ft 1in)*

(*right*)

DETAIL OF A PANEL, British, *c*1725–50.
Large leaf motifs worked on brown linen in couched knotted work, and surface stitchery. The piece was reputedly worked by the Duchess of Newasch and possibly by Princess Amelia, (daughter of George II) and Lady Chichester
EG 3904, 89 × 70cm (35 × 27½in)

(*below*)

SAMPLER, British, 1727.
Linen sampler decorated with bands of hollie-point and cutwork fillings; bordered by a satin-stitched acorn pattern
*EG 24 1987. 20.8cm (8in) square.
Given by Miss Hester Clough*

illustrated (EG 230 1983). Seemingly even royalty attempted to contribute to domestic decoration: a panel of knotted-work in the Collection (EG 3904) was reputedly stitched in the mid-eighteenth century by the Duchess of Newasch and Princess Amelia, daughter of George II. It is a robust piece of needlework, executed in heavy linen threads on a brownish coloured linen ground. Much of the design of large pattern-filled leaves is worked in knotted threads, couched down on to the line. This panel is only a section of the much larger original furnishing which was cut up at some time during its life.

The canvaswork panel from a chair seat (EG 3428), illustrated, also dates from the earlier eighteenth century. Such pictorial designs were applied to furnishings. Professionals and amateur embroiderers produced a variety of canvaswork in the form of wall panels, screens, carpets, table tops and cabinet panels. The popularity of padded chairs probably did much to promote canvaswork embroidery. Fully upholstered wing chairs were often embroidered with patterns of coiling plants, or flowers restrained in baskets and pots. Alternatively, the foliage may have opened out to reveal a scene of dallying rustics, or an illustration of a Bible story or classical legend. The

seats and back pads of suites of chairs provided excellent opportunities for stitching whole sequences of related scenes.

The design on this canvas chair-seat cover was almost certainly professionally drawn, but the unfinished embroidery is the work of an amateur. Mary (the name stitched into the lower right corner) has brought surface interest to the embroidery by varying the scale of her stitches. The faces and hands of the central figures are worked in small-scale tent stitch on a fine linen ground. These have been cut out and applied to the male figure, whilst the unfinished woman awaits the same treatment.

COSTUME

Some eighteenth-century paintings depict fashionable women wearing aprons. These were not worn for protec-

PANEL, possibly an apron, English, c1700–25.
Fine cotton muslin ground embroidered with cotton threads in surface darning and stem stitches with areas of pulledwork and eyelet holes. The chinoiserie design is a repeating pattern of a coiling plant supporting large ornate leaves and flowers interspersed with exotic birds and animals; a whimsical human figure appears on the left
EG 1587, 48.5 × 55cm (1ft 7in × 1ft 9½in)

tive purposes, but rather as attractive accessories. There are a number of these charming embroideries amongst the Guild's costume pieces. One of the earlier apron panels (EG 1587) is illustrated. The design of an all-over repeating tree pattern is reminiscent of seventeenth-century crewelwork designs, whilst the exotic birds and 'oriental' figures illustrate the taste for chinoiserie which flourished in Europe during the eighteenth century and is also seen on one of the Guild's waistcoats (EG 2324), see Chapter 4.

Short aprons with straight or scalloped edges, cut from

FLORAL PICTURE, English, c1700–50.
Linen canvas embroidered with silk threads. The vase, flower heads, leaves and stems are worked largely in tent stitch with some cross-stitched leaves. The background is worked in cream silk in Hungarian stitch, the insects are tent stitch, and the hillock uses tent and cross stitches *EG 230 1983, 19 × 20.5cm (7½ × 8in). Bequest of Miss C. M. Irons*

CHAIR SEAT (unfinished),
English, c1700–25.
The canvaswork seatcover
depicts figures in a rural setting.
The design has been drawn on
canvas and the faces and hands of
the main couple are worked
separately in a much finer stitch.
The man's face has been cut out
and applied to give a raised effect;
the woman's face and hands have
been drawn and partially stitched
on a separate piece of canvas,
waiting to be cut out and applied
to the main design
*EG 3428, 56 × 57cm (1ft 9¾in ×
1ft 10¼in). Given by Mrs Hill*

silk lengths and embroidered with coloured silk and metal threads were also popular during the early to mid-decades of the century. The Collection houses a number of these colourful pieces, most of which were probably stitched by ladies for their own use. Long cotton muslin aprons in the Collection, embroidered with whitework sprigs and floral trails, suggest work produced by commercial workshops later in the century. A detail of one of these aprons (EG 2126) is illustrated. The flower heads and cartouches are decorated with ornate pulledwork filling patterns whilst the outlines and linking stems are worked in tamboured chain stitch.

Tambourwork was a technique brought to Europe from the Orient during the mid-eighteenth century. The technique is given a French name to describe the method of stretching the ground fabric taut through a frame to form a drum-like surface. A hook is inserted through the fabric from above to catch the embroidery thread held below. Then the thread is brought to the surface and the action repeated. Gradually a line of looped chain stitches is formed on the surface. The technique

was popular as a form of leisure embroidery but the commercial advantages of such a speedy method were soon utilised by professionals. The most famous amongst these was Luigi Ruffini, an Italian immigrant who established a commercial embroidery workshop in Edinburgh in 1782.

Throughout most of the eighteenth century, lace retained its position as a fashionable but expensive costume accessory. The Guild Collection contains examples of an exquisitely pretty form of embroidery which developed as a competitor to the most expensive bobbinlaces. This embroidery emerged during the early eighteenth century as a popular alternative to lace. Originally it was commercially produced in Saxony, and is thus sometimes called '*point de Saxe*'; more usually the technique is referred to as 'Dresdenwork' since most of the embroidery was exported from that area by merchants (see *Lace: A History* by Santina Levey). The lacy effects were achieved by pulled stitchery in a variety of complicated patterns, with surface stitchery and shadow work emulating the denser areas of bobbinlace clothwork. Originally,

(right)

Apron (detail), British or European, mid-eighteenth to late eighteenth century. The apron, which would have been worn as a fashion accessory, is in cotton muslin embroidered with cotton thread in tamboured chain stitch with pulledwork fillings. The rococo cartouches are filled with a variety of chain stitch which is also used to work the plant stems, leaves and petals
EG 2126. 98 × 130cm (3ft 2¼in × 4ft 2¾in)

(opposite)

Waistcoat, English, c1730–40.
The white linen waistcoat, embroidered with white linen thread in a variety of stitches including pulledwork, satin stitch, and French knots, is an example of professional work. The design is similar to that seen in Dresdenwork of the period, and both derive their patterns from contemporary laces
EG 2467, length 73cm (2ft 4½in). Given by Miss Martineau

(*right*)

Mᴬᴺ'ˢ ˢᵁᴵᵀ, English or European, *c*1770–90. The coat and breeches are made from purple and green, cut and uncut velvet. The silk satin waistcoat fronts are heavily embroidered with a stylised floral design in silks, in long and short, satin and stem stitches, with coiled metal wire. The same design, techniques and threads decorate the coat fronts, pocket, skirt, tail and cuffs. The detail shows the coat back. This sumptuous outfit, professionally tailored and embroidered, would have been worn on formal occasions. The pocket lining of the breeches is inscribed in ink 'Marquess of Hartington' (son of the Duke of Devonshire, Chatsworth House)
EG 441–443, coat length 104cm (3ft 4½in)

Sᵀᴼᴹᴬᶜᴴᴱᴿ ᴬᴺᴰ Qᵁᴵᴸᵀᴱᴰ petticoat, English mid-eighteenth century. The stomacher, stiffened by a centrally placed horn busk, is fine linen embroidered with floss silks in long and short stitches and couched metal threads. The meandering background pattern formed with couched metal threads imitates a quilting design.

The petticoat of green silk satin is lined with coarsely woven linen, wadded with sheepswool and quilted throughout
Stomacher: EG 24 1981, 34 × 25cm (1ft 1¼in × 9¾in). Given by Lady Adam Gordon
Petticoat: EG 3882, 94 × 305cm (36½in × 10ft). Given by the Duchess of Portland

locally available linen threads and linen ground fabrics would have been used, but these were quickly supplemented, then replaced, by imported cotton yarns and muslins. During the first half of the eighteenth century, Dresdenwork became internationally fashionable. The pieces shown here illustrate its most popular use as a costume trimming.

The pieces of Dresdenwork illustrated (EG 3097, EG 8 1981) are composed of large, patterned, floral shapes, reminiscent of contemporary lace and figured silks. They are also seen in men's whitework waistcoats such as the one illustrated (EG 2467).

During the eighteenth century, men's court and formal costume was particularly lavish. Coats and breeches were cut from sumptuous, perhaps figured, silks and velvets against which ornately embroidered waistcoats glittered and gleamed. A most opulent example in the Collection is the splendid outfit illustrated (EG 441–443). The soft silk velvet coat and breeches contrast with a gleaming ivory satin waistcoat. Both coat and waistcoat are embroidered with silk and metal threads in a stylised floral pattern. Informal wear was more restrained but not necessarily less finely made. The whitework waistcoat mentioned above is an example of fashionable informal wear c1730–40. The embroidery is obviously professional work. The pattern of exotic flowers is richly textured through the use of

TWO FICHUS, European, first half of the eighteenth century.
White cotton ground fabrics embroidered with white linen thread. The top example of Dresdenwork incorporated

shadow work to create the effect of the cloth areas of bobbinlace
Top: EG 3097, 72cm (2ft 4in) each side. Given by Miss J. M. Bower. EG 8 1981, 74cm (2ft 5in) each side. Given by Mrs R. Watson

pulledwork and various surface stitches. Other whitework waistcoats (not illustrated) in the Collection demonstrate the use of stuffed and corded quilting to bring similar designs into relief. The front panel of these waistcoats was obviously the focus of attention. Being aware of this the tailors constructed the normally unseen reverse parts from coarser materials.

Quilting was also used in women's costume. The informal but fashionable petticoat illustrated (EG 3882) is comprised of three layers: a surface of fine silk satin, a filling of sheepswool, and a coarse linen lining. The 'sandwich' is unified by lines of stitches worked in a decorative pattern, a border of stylised flowers and an all-over diamond mesh. The petticoats of the overdress may have been worn parted to reveal this attractive draught excluder. The stomacher, illustrated with the petticoat, has a meandering background pattern formed with couched metal threads in imitation of quilting.

VICTORIAN EMBROIDERY

During the nineteenth century, embroidery was pursued with great enthusiasm by a growing number of comfortably affluent leisured ladies. A treasury of nineteenth-century work is housed in the Guild Collection as evidence of their passion. However, no one technique appears to have surpassed Berlinwork in popularity.

Berlinwork was embroidery carried out mainly in wools on canvas. The designs were copied from patterns printed on to squared paper and hand painted. Each square on the paper represented one stitch on the canvas. At its height of popularity in the middle of the nineteenth century, Berlinwork was used to create and decorate all manner of objects ranging through pictorial panels, a variety of furnishing pieces and costume. According to nineteenth-century authors, the patterns were first published in Berlin in 1804 or 1805 by a printseller called Philipson. As the vogue for Berlinwork developed, other publishers followed suit, issuing their own patterns, firstly in Germany and then internationally. The Collection contains examples printed in Germany, Austria, France and England. In Britain the technique was greatly boosted by the opening of commercial outlets for imported patterns, canvases and wools. The first and most famous was opened by Mr Wilks in 1831 at 136 Regent Street, London.

Canvases were manufactured in various materials, gauges and colours. The great appeal of Berlinwork no doubt stemmed in part from its relative simplicity. One unfinished panel in the Collection (EG 3509), not illustrated, demonstrates a way in which amateur embroiderers were assisted: the embroidery is worked on white cotton canvas with every tenth thread coloured yellow to facilitate counting.

The woollen yarns used for Berlinwork were known as Berlin, zephyr, merino or German wools. These soft pliable yarns formed from the fleece of the merino sheep were initially spun in Gotha and dyed in Berlin. From the mid-century the wools used were usually brightly coloured with the newly developed chemical dyes. These were evidently admired by embroiderers who found them most suitable for copying vivid designs of exotic blooms and birds. Berlinwork stitched during the late-1850s and 1860s demonstrates a particularly flamboyant use of colour and stitch. The parrot panel illustrated (EG 3794) is an excellent example, showing all the hallmarks of Berlinwork at its height of popularity, c1860. The flowers, fruit and foliage are worked in cross stitch, a simple technique but one of the most popular in the Berlinwork embroiderer's repertoire. A large-scale variant called

'Leviathan stitch' was also known as 'railway stitch' because it covered the ground so quickly (*The Dictionary of Needlework* Caulfield and Saward, 1882). The startling parrot was given his three-dimensional form through the use of plush stitch, also known as velvet stitch, which was particularly popular during the mid-century decades. It is formed by working lines of loops and securing these in place by cross or tent stitches; the loops are then cut and clipped to different heights to create the desired sculptural form.

Large exotic flowers, like those seen in the parrot panel, were also particularly popular during the 1850s and 1860s. There are a number of pieces in the Collection where the overblown nature of the flowers has been greatly emphasised by the use of plush stitch worked in luridly coloured wools.

During the 1850s beadwork became popular. Some of these pieces combine wool embroidery with beads. Occasionally brass and faceted steel beads were used, but the main trend was for clear and coloured glass in white, black and shades of grey to create tonal beadwork known as 'grisaille work'. The angel panel illustrated (EG 5731), which uses glass beads, may have been intended as a firescreen where the beads would have glinted in the firelight. In several ornamental panels such as this no attempt has been made to work the background. It was fashionable to leave close-meshed silk canvases unworked in order to enjoy their shimmering surface.

Berlin designs were derived from many sources. Illustrated publications such as Audubon's *Birds of America* (1827–38) and Gould's *Birds of Australia* (1837–8) provided models for the popular bird designs. Pictorial pieces reveal a taste for romantic and sentimental themes, whilst biblical scenes continued in popularity. Barbara Morris (see Bibliography) has described how at the Great Exhibition of 1851 six embroidered interpretations of Leonardo da Vinci's 'Last Supper' were exhibited. The habit of copying directly from paintings, prints and engravings, or adapting them in some way was permitted without restriction until the Registration of Designs Act in 1842. This abundance of freely available design material encouraged the production of Berlin patterns. By 1840 14,000 different designs had been recorded (see *Victorian Canvas Work* M. G. Proctor).

Despite Berlinwork's wide appeal, needlework books and women's magazines advised adventurous spirits on the use of a variety of materials and techniques. The assortment of novelty items created were most aptly classified as fancywork.

(*left*)

BEADWORK PICTURE or firescreen panel, 'Day: Aurora with the Genius of Light', English *c*1860.
Double canvas worked largely in grey, white, black and clear glass beads, with some metal beads to create a grisaille effect. Brown silks are used for the hair whilst the limbs have been tent stitched and then painted
EG 5731. 62.5 × 59cm (2ft ½in × 1ft 11in)

(*above*)

PLUSHWORK PARROT PANEL, English *c*1850s–60s.
Canvas embroidered in aniline-dyed Berlin wools in cross stitch and plushwork. The loops of plush stitch are secured by cross stitches and when the work is completed the loops are cut and the fibres brushed and sheared to the required shape and height
EG 3794. 80 × 62cm (2ft 7¼in × 2ft). Given by Miss Dale

(*right*)

BERLINWORK – the most popular form of Victorian embroidery. A variety of charts, samplers and slippertop, European, *c*1840–60.
The charts include hand-coloured versions issued in Germany and a printed version from the *Young Ladies' Journal.* The vibrant coloured designs depicting exotic birds and overblown blooms are typical of Berlinwork

(right)

MOUNTMELLICK WORK sachet, English or Irish, mid-nineteenth century. Cotton ground fabric embroidered and fringed with thick, soft, cotton yarn in a typical Mountmellick work design of highly textural bramble sprays and hedgerow flowers
EG 4067. 43 × 54cm (1ft 4¾in × 1ft 9in). Given by Miss Brunskill

(opposite)

CARRICKMACROSS FAN LEAF, English or Irish, c1900. Cotton applied to a ground of machine-made lace. The design is outlined with a couched cord and the areas of pattern highlighted by needlelace fillings
EG L1049, 16 × 46.5cm (6¼in × 1ft 6in) (Photograph: Dudley Moss)

The Dictionary of Needlework, An Encyclopaedia of Artistic, Plain and Fancy Needlework published in 1882, and already mentioned, lists an extensive choice of conventional and unusual embroidery materials and techniques. Several of those recommended are represented in the Collection. The authors, Sophia Caulfield and Blanche Saward, described the use of plaited woodchips or shavings as embroidery ground. Illustrated is a panel of black net embroidered with straw. The fragment was probably cut from an early-nineteenth-century veil or dress trimming. Also pictured are fish scales, used to create three-dimensional flowerheads and stitched to a maroon velvet panel (EG 301). Not surprisingly fragile fish scales were recommended for use where friction was unlikely to occur. Preparation involved scraping the scales from the body of a carp, perch or goldfish, soaking, perforating and, if desired, tinting them with a mixture of varnish and powdered colours.

Narrow ribbons and crêpe provided odourless alternatives for working raised motifs. The cream satin reticule is an example of 1830s' crêpework. The crêpe, now faded, was folded and applied to form three-dimensional roses set against silk and chenille embroidered buds and leaves. The little Berlin bag (EG 13 1983) illustrates imaginative stitchery imitating lace. This clever surface stitchery is sometimes found on Berlinwork samplers, or incorporated into completed pieces.

Patchwork quilts were produced in Britain during the nineteenth century as a pleasurable pastime, not from

necessity – witness the printed instructions in books aimed at the leisured and affluent, and the materials used. During the first half of the nineteenth century fashionable printed cottons were the most common fabrics used in patchwork, and often in such tiny pieces that the necessarily long and laborious work would not suggest a worker in hasty need of warmth. Richly coloured dress silks and furnishing fabrics were pieced to form the tops in later decades. One sumptuous, unlined top was pieced in a diamond box pattern with a star border from coloured and black, plain and patterned silks.

It was given to the Guild by Queen Mary and is the work of her mother, the Duchess of Teck, a lady who did not need to make her own bedcovers. A large quilt of similar design illustrated on page 11 (EG 2549) employs the popular 'tumbling blocks' pattern to create an illusion of three dimensions.

The Mountmellick work (EG 4067) and Carrickmacross work (EG L1049) shown here represent two techniques used both for charitable purposes and by amateur embroideresses for pleasure. Mountmellick embroidery was reputedly developed in Mountmellick, Ireland, in the early nineteenth century, and was revived for philanthropic purposes in 1880 by a Mrs Millner. She established the Mountmellick Industrial Society in order to assist distressed gentlewomen. The popularity of the technique was no doubt boosted when the Princess of Wales was presented with a Mountmellick-embroidered dressing-tablecover on her visit to Ireland in 1885.

Characteristically, the embroidery was worked in thick white cotton yarns on heavy cotton satin ground, often fringed with cotton yarns. It was used to decorate mats, bags and covers, popular patterns being bramble and fuchsia sprays, wheatears and acorns. The heavy yarns lent themselves to raised embroidery in French knots and bullion and padded satin stitches.

After the great Irish Famine of 1846 Carrickmacross embroidery was produced and sold in attempts to alleviate the distress of local poor. It is an appliqué technique which grounds white muslin motifs on to machine-made net foundation. The invention of the machine bobbinet in 1808, and subsequent technical developments fostered the growth of such work, with industries at Coggeshall, Limerick and Nottingham among others. The largest, most famous commercial enterprise dependent upon hand embroidery was the Ayrshire trade. As the name suggests, it developed in the south-west corner of Scotland, and it flourished during the first half of the nineteenth century. Various factors contributed to the mid-century decline of this once-booming industry, the most important being developments in machine embroidery. A feature of Ayrshire whitework was the hand-made needlelace fillings popularly used in floral patterns decorating women's costume accessories and baby robes. The Guild has an extensive collection of christening and baby robes decorated with Ayrshire and other whitework techniques. An example (EG 456) is illustrated on page 45. Such garments survive because of sentimental value.

The ladies who tackled fancywork no doubt admired art needlework. Caulfield and Saward described this later-nineteenth-century craze as:

> . . . a general term for all descriptions of needlework that spring from the application of a knowledge of design and colouring, with skill in fitting and executing. It is either executed by the worker from his or her design or the patterns are drawn by a skilled artist, and much individual scope in execution and colouring is required from the embroiderers. The term is chiefly used to denote inlaid and onlaid appliqué embroidery in silk and crewels for ordinary domestic purposes, and embroidery with gold, silver and silk for churchwork, but there is no limit to its application.

The embroideries of the Royal School of Art Needlework epitomised this type of work. The School was founded in 1872 with the dual aims of raising the status of embroidery design and technique and providing employment to ladies in reduced circumstances. Leading contemporary artists including William Morris, Burne-Jones and Walter Crane were commissioned by the School to produce embroidery designs. The School's royal patronage and the involvement of eminent artists helped the aim of elevating the status of embroidery.

Several groups followed the trends set by the Royal School; occasionally the materials and techniques used identify a piece as being the work of a particular group. In the Guild collection there are three pieces of Leek

B AGS, PURSES AND COSTUME
fragments embroidered in a
variety of techniques
popular in Britain during the mid-
Victorian period.
(*top left*) The bag, *c*1830, in silk
satin is embroidered with couched
chenille threads and applied fine
cotton gauze
(*top right*) The bag in linen
canvas is embroidered with silk
and wool threads with faceted
steel bead highlights
(*centre*) Canvaswork purse in fine
wool thread
(*below*) The lower three bags use
decorative beads. The one
embroidered in white and grey
seems to imitate the North
American Indian surface technique
which had a growing novelty
value. The long purse, also known
as a 'miser's purse', was for
holding coins in the square or
rounded end according to
denomination. The fragment on
the lower left uses fish scales
stitched to a velvet ground to
form flower petals, and in the top
right corner is an example of
straw used as an embroidery
thread on net
*Size examples: fish scale panel EG
301, 21 × 54cm (8in × 1ft 9in);
bag, top right, EG 13 1983, 10 ×
13cm (4 × 5in)*

(*left*)

AYRSHIRE BABY'S ROBE (detail from the skirt), Scottish mid-nineteenth century. White cotton lawn embroidered in white cotton threads. Pulledwork and needlelace are used to create a variety of patterned fillings for the design which uses floral and rococo motifs. The pattern is echoed on the central triangular bodice panel
EG 456. 107.8cm (3ft 6in) shoulder to hem. Given by Miss Martin

(*above*)

FISHERTON INDUSTRIES reticella cover, English, early twentieth century. Unbleached linen ground decorated with cutwork and reticella motifs worked in naturally coloured linen threads
EG 5022. 180 × 100cm (5ft 10¼in × 3ft 3in). Given by Miss Beale

represent the type of part-worked embroidery which could be purchased from Morris & Co for completion at home. Their designs have a vaguely oriental flavour reflecting a growing late-nineteenth-century taste. Plants and flowers remained popular subjects for embroidery but elegant irises, trailing honeysuckle, tulips, poppies and sunflowers stitched in softly shaded silks and worsteds replaced the robust aniline blooms of the 1850s, and ascetic cranes and stately peacocks were preferred to the cut-pile parrot.

A vogue for historical design revived interest in seventeenth-century crewelwork, reinterpreted under the term Jacobean embroidery.

Towards the end of the century numerous groups adhering to the guiding principles of the Arts and Crafts movement revived traditional pre-machine-age methods and materials to create a variety of craft objects. The reticella panel illustrated (EG 5022) was a product of one of these groups. In 1902 the Fisherton Industries were set up by Josephine Newall in the Wiltshire village of Fisherton de la Mere. The work produced was characterised by cutwork and reticella motifs derived from seventeenth-century patterns and Greek embroidery. In Ireland in 1883 the Donegal Industrial Fund had

embroidery, one of which is illustrated (EG 5424). The Leek Embroidery Society was founded in 1879 by Elizabeth Wardle, wife of Thomas Wardle, a Leek silk printer and dyer. Characteristically the embroidery employed printed silk fabrics as the patterned ground, the printed outlines being covered by stitchery in rich materials such as floss silks and Japanese gold threads.

William Morris's decorative arts firm Morris & Co completed commissions and produced work for sale through its shop. Materials and patterns were also sold. The two furnishing panels illustrated (EG 3594, EG 3854) probably

(left)

TUNIC AND BOOKCOVERS showing the influence of the Arts and Crafts Movement.
The linen tunic, designed and worked by Joan Drew, is embroidered with silk threads. The Bible cover (*above*), in natural linen with floss silks and Japanese gold thread, was designed and embroidered by Nancy Clay *c*1926 while she was a student of Katherine Harris at the Royal College of Art. The bookcover (*below*) in natural linen embroidered with floss silks was worked by Louisa Pesel from an early-sixteenth-century printed design
Tunic: EG 4773, 78cm (2ft 6½in) neck to hem. Given by Miss Aldworth. Bible cover: EG 161 1983, 18 × 13cm (7 × 5in). Given by Mrs Nancy Stansfield. Bookcover: EG 597, 21 × 15cm (8 × 6in)

(right)

TWO WILLIAM MORRIS hangings, English, late nineteenth century.
Cotton and linen ground fabrics embroidered with heavy, loosely twisted silks in stem and darning stitches. Both pieces are characteristic of the work produced by the Morris & Co workrooms in the late nineteenth century. The rust-coloured panel called 'Parrot Tulip' was designed by John Henry Dearle. The other panel dates from *c*1890 to 1895
EG 3594, 52 × 132cm (1ft 8¼in × 4ft 3½in). Given by Lady Studholme. EG 3854, 92 × 59cm (3ft × 1ft 11in)

(left)

LEEK EMBROIDERY PANEL, English, *c*1880–5.
Yellow silk embroidered with silks, fine wools and couched gold threads in a characteristic Leek embroidery design
EG 5424, 17 × 21cm (6½ × 8in). Given by Miss Hyde

LINEN CURTAINS by Grace Christie and a panel of Kells embroidery, English and Irish, late nineteenth to early twentieth century.
The linen curtains, designed and worked by Grace Christie, are decorated with ribbons and embroidery in various intersecting stitches, some of which are worked over padding. The border of Kells embroidery is worked in fine wools
EG 2546 and 2545, 180 × 63cm (5ft 10¼in × 2ft ½in) and 110 × 61cm (3ft 7in × 1ft 11¾in). Given by the NFWI. EG 5733, 25.5 × 130cm (10in × 4ft 2¾in)

been established by Mrs Ernest Hart to alleviate distress from the 1880 famine by reviving traditional textile crafts including embroidery. One form promoted by the Fund became known as Kells embroidery because it derived many of its motifs of real and mythical birds and beasts and knotted strapwork patterns from Celtic manuscripts. Linen embroidery threads and linen grounds were originally used in order to stimulate the local linen industry. The Langdale Linen Industry was established in 1885 by Albert Fleming for similar purposes. A little later, embroidered decoration, again using techniques and patterns drawn from seventeenth-century reticellawork models, was introduced. This has become known as Ruskin lace, after the artist John Ruskin who helped to develop these industries.

Several embroideries from the Guild Collection are pictured to illustrate the range of work produced under the influence of the Arts and Crafts movement (EG 2546, 2545, 5733, 4773, 161 1983, 597, 4636).

ARTS AND CRAFTS STYLE bedcover, English, c1910–20. Natural linen embroidered with woollen yarns in long and short, stem, herringbone, chain and straight stitches, with French knots. 'I know a bank whereon the wild thyme blows' is stitched above and below a panel with floral sprays reminiscent of seventeenth-century sprigs, while the border is a meandering flower pattern
EG 4636, 214 × 163cm (6ft 11½in × 5ft 3½in). Given by Mrs B. Dakin

EMBROIDERY THIS CENTURY

Contemporary embroidery is exciting. Newcomers to the medium may find today's work surprising, perhaps even controversial. In recent years many embroiderers have taken an experimental approach to technique and to the choice and use of materials, to create pieces which challenge a traditional definition of embroidery – the decoration of a woven textile surface with needlework using spun threads and yarns.

A strength of the Guild Collection is its holding of twentieth-century embroidery, which includes many important progressive pieces, is rich in examples of traditional and innovative embroidery, and vividly illustrates the history of the medium during the twentieth century.

Until recent years the majority of acquisitions were donations from the membership; frequently the modern embroideries had been worked by the donors themselves, their family or friends. Some of the embroideries are good illustrations of episodes in the history of design, their motifs and patterns quite evidently inspired by a style fashionable or newly developing at the time. Many other pieces show how once-progressive styles have been adapted to suit more conservative tastes. Although these pieces are not milestones in embroidery or design history, they are very often expertly worked. Thus, while undoubtedly valuable to the social historian, they are also of interest to the technician. In recent years there has been a surge of interest in embroidery from collectors and interior designers which has enabled many embroiderers to profit by their creativity and has stimulated the production of embroidery on a professional basis. For the Guild it has inevitably meant that most of the latest acquisitions have been purchases.

Embroidery is an ornamental medium and one of its most enduring uses has been to decorate furnishings and furniture, as the Guild Collection will testify. In this context, embroidered pieces often formed part of a wider decorative style. During the opening decades of this century, most embroiderers felt that only the richest and most beautiful materials were appropriate for embroidery. A good example in the Collection is the five-panelled folding screen illustrated (EG 8 1990) embroidered

ART NOUVEAU SCREEN, English, c1900.
Natural linen embroidered with floss silk in green, grey, blue, orange and tan, using long and short, satin, whipped and couched stitch. The sinuous art nouveau design is repeated in each of the screen's five panels and the embroidery design is echoed in the decorative woodwork
EG 8 1990, each panel 182 × 58cm (5ft 11in × 1ft 10½in)
(Photograph: Embroiderers' Guild)

'MARY, MARY, QUITE contrary' handscreen designed and worked by Katherine Powell, English, 1910. The design, in laidwork, stem stitch, darning and satin stitch, is completely reversible. The lettering is shadow work. The immaculately worked embroidery, reflecting the importance attached to technical excellence at this time, is all the more remarkable because Katherine Powell had only one hand
EG 3523, 44 × 23cm (1ft 5in × 9in). Given by Lady Hamilton Fairley

ART DECO POCHETTE designed and worked by Molly Booker, English, c1930s. Silk on canvas, lined with furnishing fabric. The decorative outer panel of the bag is mainly in tent stitch. Canvaswork was very popular during the 1930s when design was considered more important than technique
EG 2661, 16 × 27cm (6 × 10½in). Given by Mrs Lintell

ART DECO FIRESCREEN designed and worked by Madeleine Clifton, English, *c*1934. The linen ground is embroidered in silk threads in a variety of stitches including pattern darning and pulledwork to achieve a highly textural effect for the semi-abstract composition. Madeleine Clifton's work was well known during the 1920s and 1930s. *EG 5288, 60 × 58cm (2ft × 1ft 10½in)*

in 1910. Each of the linen panels has been embroidered with a vigorously coiling pattern of honeysuckle plants. Rhythmic, asymmetrically swirling designs such as this spring from the art nouveau style which flourished during the late nineteenth and early twentieth centuries. Its influence is apparent in several early-twentieth-century embroideries in the Collection, usually through the use of coiling plant or flower motifs.

Art nouveau's free-flowing patterns, while often based on plant forms, also use as subjects ultra-feminine, plumply pretty ladies in various stages of undress. Sumptuous working materials are suited to such a sensuous style: the embroideress who worked this screen selected heavy floss silks in shades of green and gold and worked in embroidery stitches (satin, stem and Cretan) which allowed the rich surface sheen of the silks to be enjoyed.

Technical skill was considered of the highest importance by early-twentieth-century, mainstream embroideresses. Amongst the Guild's pieces designed and worked c1910–20 are a number of pieces by Katherine Powell which illustrate this point. The handscreen illustrated (EG 3523) which depicts the nursery rhyme 'Mary, Mary, quite contrary', was submitted by Miss Powell as part of her work for the City and Guilds of London Institute examinations. The silk embroidery is meticulously and precisely worked in a range of stitches designed to display the embroiderer's prowess. Most of the stitchery is reversible, so emphasising the level of skill involved. Such an excellent piece is appropriately mounted in a fine silver frame with a handle.

In 1919 Katherine Powell was awarded the Silver Medal at the Advanced Level of the City and Guilds examinations. Rather dauntingly, the examiner on that occasion was the great authority on embroidery, Grace Christie. It is all the more remarkable that Katherine Powell was a prize-winning embroideress considering that she had only one hand.

The designs in pieces by Katherine Powell typify popular taste of the day: some of them have a sweet, whimsical quality, whilst other pieces display oriental and historic influences. A variety of embroideries in the Collection, ranging through teacosies, nightdress cases, jewellery boxes and pictorial pieces, share these styles. However, the firescreen panel illustrated (EG 5288) embroidered in about 1934 by Madeleine Clifton contrasts sharply with such work. This panel shows the influence of art deco. In 1968 Bevis Hillier (see Bibliography) settled on this term to describe 'an assertively modern style, developing in the 1920s and reaching its high point in the thirties'. The name was derived from L'Exposition International des Arts Décoratifs et Industriels Modernes, held in Paris in 1925. Art deco was a multi-faceted style with influences drawn from many sources, including the Aztec Indians,

Egypt, the Ballet Russe, the Glasgow School and the Bauhaus but, as Hillier pointed out, all aspects were united by a certain trait: the designs were symmetrical and recti-linear and 'responded to the demands of the machine and of new materials'. Clifton's arrangement of not-quite geometric shapes was obviously a response to this new style.

Figures were also a popular part of art deco, but the languid ladies of art nouveau were transformed into muscular striding women, often accompanied by straining dogs. In the Collection an appliqué panel (not illustrated) by Barbara Snook depicts a pinkly naked lady dancing through an arrangement of applied shapes: she is a softer version of the newly athletic woman. Another panel (not illustrated), also worked in appliqué, illustrates a faun, cut from kid leather, and stitched against a stylised forest background. Clifton's exotic palm-tree design (on the illustrated firescreen) is an interesting move away from the popular English cottage garden and coincides with our image of the sophisticated, racy and cosmopolitan 1930s.

Canvaswork continued to be popular during the 1930s when designs by leading artists were often worked by amateurs. However, Molly Booker appears to have embroidered the pochette (EG 2661) herself, with tigers and a village scene.

Of course, not all embroiderers at this time were enthusiasts of modern style. The Collection contains many examples of embroideries which use more traditional designs. These were usually worked by women for whom embroidery was a hobby. The more progressive styles and techniques tended to be used by embroidery students and professionals.

Madeleine Clifton's firescreen panel is an example of the work of the designer-embroiderer who understands the needs and potential of the medium and the materials for which she is designing. During the 1930s there seems to have been a brief vogue for artists to produce designs to be worked by embroiderers. The work tended to be executed in simple canvaswork techniques, lacking textural interest, and did not achieve the success of Madeleine Clifton's piece. Clifton's clever use of pulledwork and darning stitches added texture and surface pattern to the design; the effect of the stitchery lifted the work beyond similar printed or painted images. The success of her work reinforced the long-held opinion that if possible the designer and the embroiderer should be one and the same.

'Chords' (EG 110 1983) is another panel which reflects this period's style. It was designed and worked by Elizabeth Grace Thomson c1934. The abstract design has an explosive quality accentuated by the use of once vibrantly coloured materials, which, sadly, have now faded to

pastel shades. The methods used in designing and executing this piece may have been taught to Thomson by Rebecca Crompton (1895–1947).

Rebecca Crompton believed that the potentials of embroidery could be most fully realised when the designer and craftsperson were the same. In 1936 she published her approach in *Modern Design in Embroidery*. Aware that many people had limited drawing skills, she gave instruction on how to design through the arrangement of cut and torn fabric shapes and additional three-dimensional objects such as buttons and sequins. In subsequent years this method of designing became a

MACHINE-EMBROIDERED mat designed and probably worked by Rebecca Crompton, English, 1938. Rayon organdie embroidered with cutwork and machine-made needlelace fillings in cotton and metal thread. A fine example of early machine embroidery
EG 1046. 16 × 15cm (6¼ × 6in). Given by the NDS

standard approach. It is apparent in 'Chords', which is formed from arranging and layering fabric shapes, with the design emphasised by surface stitchery in silk and metal threads, ribbons and cords. Such a spontaneous approach to design and freer use of materials is in

'GERANIUMS' PANEL designed and worked by Richard Box. English, 1986. The panel is built up with mixed fabrics through collage and appliqué techniques using machine and hand embroidery to secure pieces and bring a high surface texture to the work *EG 6 1990, 142 × 104cm (4ft 7½in × 3ft 4½in). Purchased*

'CHORDS' PANEL designed and worked by Elizabeth Grace Thomson, English, 1934. Mixed fabrics and threads including silks, chiffon and gauze, satin, velvet and Lurex. Fabric shapes have been inlaid and applied to a striped ground fabric, and the design emphasised by surface stitchery including satin stitch, couching, cross stitch, buttonholing and individual chain stitches using floss and twisted silks, ribbons, metal cords and threads *EG 110 1983, 90 × 88cm (2ft 11in × 2ft 10¼in). Bequest of Elizabeth Grace Thomson*

'TRANQUIL FIGURE' PANEL designed and worked by Alice Kettle, English, 1987. Felted fabric machine stitched with silk, metal and cotton threads. The three-dimensional effects have been achieved by manipulating and moulding the ground felt with tension stitchery. The stitches are laid down in patches and layers of colour. The depth, solidity and texture is in complete contrast to the light surface sketches created with machine embroidery in the 1930s (see picture page 53)
EG 8 1988, 58 × 77cm (1ft 10½in × 2ft 6in). Purchased

marked contrast to the control and precision displayed in Katherine Powell's embroidery .

The dynamism and colour of 'Chords' seems totally appropriate to the period now often referred to as the 'Jazz Age'. A smaller panel (not illustrated) in the Collection was also worked by one of Crompton's students, Miss E. Griffiths. It is a piece in the design stage, showing the method of working quickly with cut fabric shapes. In this case they are cut from dress and furnishing fabrics which have been glued and held into place by long straight stitches, with randomly placed metal sequins. The panel represents two figures in the rain with an umbrella.

The Guild owns only one piece of embroidery catalogued as being by Rebecca Crompton herself (EG 1046), page 53. In contrast to the pieces described so far, this is machine rather than hand embroidered. Designing for machine mass-production was a general concern of the 1930s but one which was largely rejected by embroiderers.

In 1934 the embroiderer Eleanor French expressed her view that embroidery was stagnating, partly because of a widespread reliance on transfer patterns, but primarily because of the absence of any mechanical developments which would stimulate technical innovation. In the absence of such developments repetitious traditional methods continued. Until the 1930s sewing machines had been used largely to imitate cheaply and speedily the effects of hand embroidery; the creative potential of the machine was not recognised. Rebecca Crompton and Dorothy Benson were key figures in revolutionising the situation. Benson was a skilled technician and had been employed by the Singer Sewing Machine Company since 1916. Crompton and Benson were introduced to each other by Elizabeth Thomson, and the two women formed a working alliance to investigate the creative possibilities of the domestic sewing machine. Today, when machine embroidery is more widely accepted than ever before as a creative medium, it is surprising to learn of the negative response the demonstration lectures given by the duo sometimes received. Joan Edwards has recorded how groups of teachers left before the sessions ended as a comment on their content.

Eventually Crompton and Benson prevailed and brought creative embroidery into the machine age. Crompton's mat typifies the work they popularised. She had been swift to appreciate the sewing machine as a means of executing her dynamic designs. Even where static figures formed a part of the design as in this piece a sense of unity and movement could be injected through the use of scrolling lines.

The shimmering transparent materials (silks, chiffons, organzas, rayon organza) and metal threads used in 'Chords' and Crompton's mat reflect the popularity during the 1930s of luxurious materials. It is also interesting to note that Crompton and Thomson used synthetic and newly developed materials such as rayon and Lurex, popular as a novelty and as symbols of a truly modern style.

World War II brought restrictions and a limited supply of embroidery materials, but proved an unexpected spur to the creation of experimental embroidery. Necessity compelled needlewomen to make the most use of fabric supplies. The groundwork for experimenting with fabric, exploring the complementary and contrasting qualities of patterns and textures had been laid in the 1930s. Unwittingly the hard-pressed wartime housewives and embroiderers were developing this trend.

In post-war years the Needlework Development Scheme (NDS) continued to promote good design and technique in embroidery. The Scheme had been founded in 1934, and hoped to achieve its aims through publications, lectures, exhibitions and the circulation of a collection of its inspirational embroideries. When it closed in 1962 the Scheme had amassed a collection of 3,500 historic and contemporary, British and foreign embroideries. Of these, 473 were transferred to the Embroiderers' Guild Collection. The majority of these pieces date from the 1940s to the 1960s. The cotcover illustrated (EG 826) was commissioned by the NDS from Winsome Douglass, an embroiderer and teacher who created many pieces for the Scheme.

The Guild now houses several of the highly characteristic embroideries which she worked for the NDS. Douglass frequently mixed ground materials in contrasting primary colours and textures – red and black were particular favourites – and created additional textural surface pattern through the use of a variety of hand-made stitches. NDS commissions often used widely available, easy-to-manipulate materials such as towelling, felt and gingham. Newcomers to embroidery and children, a major target area for the NDS, would have been intimidated by expensive silks liable to slip or fray. Remember too that rationing did not end until the 1950s. Many NDS pieces now in the Guild Collection make use of ground fabrics with a printed or woven pattern. These were intended to be used by the students as a springboard to

'THE KING' COTCOVER designed and worked by Winsome Douglass, English, 1951.
Red and cream woollen flannel is pieced to form the background which is embroidered with silks in various stitches. The cover was commissioned by the Needlework Development Scheme from Winsome Douglass who made great use of varied hand stitchery and the contrast and interplay between ground fabrics, fabrics and stitchery, and took care to match the design to the form and function of the piece
EG 826, 76 × 51cm (2ft 5½in × 1ft 8in). Given by the NDS

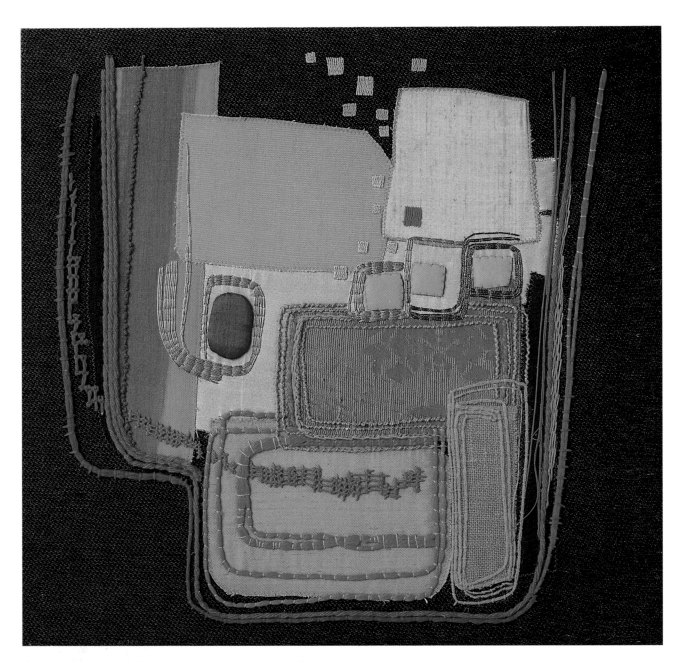

'FIRE GLOW' PANEL designed and worked by Constance Howard, English, c1967. Wool, cotton, silk and synthetic furnishing fabric embroidered with woollen yarns and silk threads. The composition is formed through application of fabric shapes, sometimes over padding, to a furnishing-fabric ground. Surface embroidery is in couching, knot, Cretan and raised chain stitches. Constance Howard MBE ARCA ATD FSD was Principal Lecturer in Charge of Textiles and Embroidery at Goldsmith's School of Art, University of London, 1947–75. Her progressive work and teaching have made her a leading, highly influential figure in modern embroidery. She is also an authority and prolific author on historical and contemporary embroidery

EG 928, 59cm (1ft 11in) square. Purchased

'SILVER SUPERSHEEP' PANEL
designed and worked by
Heather Clarke, English,
1973.
The sheep are worked in crochet
and looped stitches with tent-
stitch legs and heads. The
landscape is built up of applied
furnishing fabrics with surface
stitchery and the sky is made from
metallised card
*EG 4369, 49.5 × 49cm (1ft 7¼in
× 1ft 7in)*

creating their own designs. Invariably the NDS embroideries take a practical form such as napkins and traycloths, cotcovers, aprons and clothing. A functional element was hoped to appeal to the majority of potential embroiderers. Although the NDS embroideries now seem rather homely, they are greeted with nostalgic affection by visitors to the Guild who first met the pieces either as grateful teachers or as children struggling to master the intricacies of cross stitch.

It would be extremely difficult to refute the claim that the post-war decades have been the most experimental period in the history of embroidery. These years are characterised by excitingly innovative techniques and use of materials, which have been paralleled by the growing awareness and acceptance of embroidery as an expressive art form. This dynamic period was instigated by a strong desire for change and renewal in a war-weary Britain and by a replenished and extended stock of natural and synthetic materials when rationing ended. The main impetus for creative development was channelled through the art schools. Consequently the majority of pieces acquired by the Guild to represent these developments are the work of students and professional embroiderers.

Not surprisingly, the creation of a new and modern world involved the use of new techniques. Machine embroidery began to flourish. It is possible to trace the use of the sewing machine as a creative embroidery tool from the 1940s to the 1980s through embroideries in the Guild Collection.

An early post-war example of machine embroidery in the Collection is a teacosy (see Introduction) originally owned by the NDS. It was designed by Frances Beal and worked by Dorothy Benson in 1946 on a domestic sewing machine. The light sketchy motifs became characteristic of the many linear designs of the 1950s. The machine was discovered to be invaluable in executing dynamic designs which emphasised movement, such as Joy Clucas's 'Nuclear Fission' (1962), a wall panel (not illustrated) now in the Collection. During the 1950s embroiderers gradually realised the effects which could be achieved through machine embroidery, and came to see how the mechanics of the machine could be manipulated to produce a range of free stitches, creating entirely fresh effects very different from hand embroidery. Machine embroidery designs become less skeletal and greater use of the machine was made to create textures. More recently, machines have been used to cover entirely a ground fabric. A portrait (not illustrated) by Kaye Lynch in the Collection combines all-over machine stitchery with underlying paintwork. Jeanette Pekari's panels (not illustrated) show how machines can be used to create solid patches of colour which are built up to form a densely worked design. By working over applied felts and cords she has brought areas of relief to her work. One Pekari panel – a scene of dancing figures – features an undulating ground fabric which emphasises the movement inherent in the design. The rippling effect is achieved by distorting the fabric through stitch tension.

Alice Kettle is a contemporary professional embroiderer noted for her painterly machine techniques. Indeed, she trained as a painter but chooses to work in the textile medium. 'Tranquil Figure' on page 55 (EG 8 1988) demonstrates the use of an undulating ground fabric, once again achieved through stitch tension and fabric manipulation. It is an attempt to release embroidery from a two-dimensional format. Kettle's imagery may be regarded as disturbing, but unexpected images are increasingly found in embroidery as it develops into an expressive medium.

Collage and appliqué techniques may have been boosted by shortages during the war, but there have been, and are, many contemporary embroiderers who use these techniques for aesthetic reasons. The Collection's 'Owl on a Branch' (1960s, not illustrated) by Margaret Kaye demonstrates the use of collage to produce 'movement rather than hard edged compositions of shapes with confining outlines', and she was interested in 'textural and tonal values and the effects of light', as C. Howard writes (see Bibliography). This rather impressionist use of fabrics is popular today. It is a feature of Richard Box's flower designs. 'Geraniums' on page 54 (EG 6 1990) is a large-scale panel worked as a rich collage of mixed fabric fragments which have been secured by random machine and hand stitching. The edges of the fabrics have been allowed to remain free to create a highly textured surface. The Guild owns four wall panels by Richard Box, all of which employ appliqué techniques to work figurative or floral designs.

An exploration of fabric and stitch has been a feature of post-war embroidery. Exploratory embroidery is intimately bound up with the post-war enthusiasm in art schools for creating a new art form. During the 1950s and 1960s embroidery students were encouraged to observe nature in minute, even microscopic, detail and to translate their observations into embroidery designs. Resultant work was usually abstract, often worked with a variety of stitch techniques, but dominated by the materials used. Conventional and unusual fabrics and found objects (stones, shells, buttons, beads, wood shavings etc) were applied to panels to create textural effects. These were not always successful but they continued a trend promoted by Rebecca Crompton and released embroiderers from using a limited range of conventional materials. 'Fire Glow', page 58, (EG 928) by Constance Howard is a more restrained and mature use of materials and stitch: the appliqué panel succeeds as a vibrant exploration of the colour and textural contrasts between fabrics, yarns and stitch techniques.

The effects which can be achieved through the selection and use of hand-made stitches has been the concern of many embroiderers in recent years. 'Silver Supersheep' (EG 4369) by Heather Clarke demonstrates the dense textural effects that can be created through embroidery. The piece is an example of the way contemporary embroiderers have dismissed conventions dictating where, and how, particular techniques should be used: the sheep's fleeces are worked in freely looped and crocheted stitches in appropriately thick yarns. Many embroiderers today are borrowing techniques and materials from other areas and developing them to suit their purposes. In this panel the startling silver sky is cut from 'mirror-lux' card. Another particularly modern feature of this panel is the use of colour, where the silver sky, blood-red sheep and bright blue shadow create a negative image effect and bring an unreal nightmare quality to the panel. Again, some people may not be able to reconcile this with the traditional idea of embroidery as a pleasing decorative art.

Eleri Mills has also developed hand stitchery, this time with paintwork. In the wallhangings illustrated the stitchery in crewel wools is random and free. The technique is prompted by the needs of the subject and not governed by a tradition. This free approach is shared with many contemporary embroiderers. The success of 'Jess', page 63, (EG 30 1985) relies on the balance and contrast between the paintwork and stitchery. It illustrates an important modern development, a mixing of media where the success of the work depends on all the component parts and what they can contribute to the overall effect. If one material or technique is removed then the effectiveness of the work is diminished.

Many embroiderers have been incorporating paintwork into their pieces since the early 1980s. Verina Warren is noted for her depictions of the countryside which use paintwork with hand and machine embroidery, as in 'Landscape' (not illustrated), a panel by Warren now in the Collection. Her style is very different from that of Eleri Mills: the paintwork is precise and detailed, and she uses machine stitchery to create tightly knotted areas representing trees, bushes and so on; these contrast sharply with the sweeping, random hand stitches employed by Mills. The work of the two women is yet another example of how varied and individual contemporary embroidery can be.

If mixing stitchery with hand-painted and stencilled, sprayed and dyed fabrics has become a feature of 1980s' embroidery, then another hallmark of the decade has been the way in which embroiderers have mixed and manipulated unusual materials and techniques. Inevitably after four decades of exploring and exploiting the properties of available materials, embroiderers have become interested in producing their own embroidery materials. In some cases this has been by degrading what already exists, or by creating a new material such as hand-made paper and felt. These materials have inspired embroiderers over recent years particularly, and the Collection houses a number of pieces demonstrating their use. The densely layered 'Four Elements', page 62, (EG 32 1985) by Jean Draper includes sheets of book muslin which have been burnt to create a random line and colour variation. A cluster of shiny ribbons and natural and waxed linen threads have been trapped beneath stitches and randomly cut to create a lively three-dimensional area.

Contemporary embroiderers have not rejected skill, but they do refuse to be limited by traditional conventions which dictate the way in which materials and techniques should be used. During this century embroidery has made tremendous advances: now, instead of following trends set by other media, embroidery is creating style itself.

'THE FOUR ELEMENTS' PANEL designed and worked by Jean Draper. English, 1982.
A three-dimensional landscape is built up through the layering of various fabrics, some of which have burnt edges. These include hand-felted fabrics, surface stitchery, string and entwined knotted shreds
EG 32 1985, 74 × 41.5cm (2ft 5in × 1ft 4¼in). Purchased (Photograph: Dudley Moss)

'JESS', TWO WALLHANGINGS, designed and worked by Eleri Mills, Welsh, 1984. The rural landscape with a collie dog in the foreground has a spray-painted background of cotton canvas, with trees, clouds and landscape emphasised in random straight stitches in crewel wools *EG 30 1985, 119.5 × 51cm (3ft 10½in × 1ft 8in) each panel. Purchased*

NORTH AMERICAN SELECTION

Indian Work and Quilts

Lynn Szygenda

THE COLLECTION HAS a number of North American pieces, examples of the textile and embroidery crafts traditionally associated with American Indians and pioneer settlers.

American Indian craftworkers have become noted for their bold and colourful blankets, and sewn and woven beadwork. The use of moosehair, porcupine and bird quills is an indigenous Indian art which utilised native materials to decorate a range of artefacts and costume pieces. These crafts required great skill, and pieces of quillwork and moosehair embroidery are eminently collectable. Three delightful birchbark boxes in the Collection were given to the Guild by Queen Mary: they are dextrously decorated with dyed moosehair embroidery in designs which show a European influence.

The American patchwork quilts in the Collection were all stitched in the nineteenth century; and all but one of them are pieced in a variation of popular star patterns. Amongst them is a quilt pieced in a Star of Bethlehem pattern from diamond-shaped patches of white and coloured cottons. It was reputedly stitched in *c*1860 by Mrs Elizabeth Kennedy, who was born in Scotland and emigrated to the United States of America where she became sewing maid to one of the Roosevelt family. When Mrs Kennedy died, the quilt was passed to her niece in Scotland, and her sister gave the quilt to the Embroiderers' Guild in 1967.

INDIAN WORK

A diversity of needlecrafts was well established in North America before the arrival of European settlers and the collection contains a small number of examples of Indian bead, quill and moosehair embroidery.

A range of Indian costume pieces and accessories, such as the glove and bag illustrated (EG 2174, 5063), was decorated with such materials. Indigenous ground materials used for needlework included animal hides and birchbark, both of which had the advantage of being supple and water repellent. The materials used to create surface decoration varied according to availability. Seeds, shells, carved bone, minerals and wampum were all stitched to form surface decoration. Wampum was the name given to purple and white cylinders, similar in appearance to bugle beads, cut from mussel shells. These would be threaded on to sinews to form short rows which would then be attached by the ends only to the ground

hide. Rather derisively this speedy technique has been called 'lazy squaw stitch'. An alternative method was to secure the row by couching along the sinew – a method suited to curvilinear patterns or outlines. When working a hide ground the sinew would catch the surface layers of

Gauntlet glove and bandolea bag, North American (Indian), nineteenth century.
The gauntlet is one of a pair cut from hide, lined with printed cottons and decorated with glass beadwork embroidery. Lazy squaw stitch is used to attach beads on the back of the hand section; the beads on the gauntlet area are tightly secured by stringing beads on a thread and firmly couching this thread to the hide.

The bag is made from black facecloth, lined with cotton twill; decorated with glass beadwork embroidery and a bead and wool tassel fringe. The beads are strung and couched along the length of the thread. White and clear beads edge the bag
Glove: EG 2174, 37cm (1ft 2½in) cuff to finger tip. Given by Miss Jenkinson
Bag: EG 5063, 41cm (1ft 4in) long. Given by Mrs Gidman
(Photograph: Peter Williams)

PATCHWORK BEDSPREAD, North American, mid-nineteenth century.
Plain and printed cotton fabrics, cotton lining, light wadding; quilted throughout. The quilt top is pieced from square and rectangular blocks of plain white cotton and eight-sided stars formed from eight large diamond shapes, which are in turn pieced from smaller diamonds of printed fabric. The plain blocks are decorated with quilted patterns of feathers and feathered circles and the stars are quilted with straight lines of running stitches
EG 2543, 226 × 232cm (7ft 4in × 7ft 6½in). Given by Mrs Parshall (Photograph: Peter Williams)

PATCHWORK BEDSPREAD, North American, nineteenth century (detail).
Pieced cotton top, lined with printed cotton, wadded and quilted. A complex arrangement of triangles of printed cotton dress fabrics is used to create a sophisticated quilt
EG 3432, 104 × 166cm (3ft 4½in × 5ft 4¾in). Given by Mrs Parshall

skin, penetrating the entire thickness at the beginning and end of each row only. This allowed the inner skin to maintain a comfortable smooth surface.

Other indigenous pliable materials were used as embroidery 'threads': grasses, porcupine and bird quills, moosehair and some other animal hairs. Quills (softened in the mouth while working) and moosehair were both dyed before use. Couching stitches were used to attach bent and flattened quills to the ground material, the couching running stitches being hidden in the folds or hinges of the quills. When fine birchbark was the ground material in use the decorative hair would be made to penetrate the bark.

The colonisation of the continent by Europeans inevitably affected the lifestyles and traditions of the Indian nations. Settlers and traders brought materials readily assimilated by many Indian craft workers. Glass and porcelain beads, known as 'pony beads', were perhaps the most notable exchange commodity.

Although first introduced to the Eastern Woodlands Indians in 1675, the beads derived the name 'pony' from the method of distribution, by pony pack trains, to the more westerly tribes of the Plains c1800–40 (Clabburn). Indian needleworkers were already using sewing techniques to attach indigenous materials; lazy squaw and couching stitches were just as suitable for securing beads.

Wampum, seeds and to a certain extent quills were supplanted by the imported beads so that beadwork is now considered a traditional Indian craft.

As well as artefacts, the settlers brought a repertoire of motifs taken from fashionable European design which eventually influenced the patterns and imagery of much native American work. Not only the appearance but the basis of production of much Indian embroidery was changed. In response to the interest in Indian novelties vast amounts of beadwork and quillwork were being stitched by the end of the nineteenth century.

Missionary groups are often cited as having the earliest, most obvious and most direct impact upon the traditional Indian work. From 1639 Ursuline nuns from a Quebec convent began teaching embroidery and needlework skills to white settlers and local Indian tribes. Although they used imported materials to teach a European embroidery tradition, indigenous materials were also used, presumably in response to shortages of silk threads and suchlike. Many existing artefacts embroidered with quill and moosehair show the influence of the Ursulines: they are frequently objects applicable to a European culture, for example cigarcases, mats, tablecovers and boxes, decorated with floral motifs and sprays similar to European pattern-sources. Two such boxes and a cigarcase are illustrated (EG 4322, 4418, 39).

QUILTS

Historically, fashionable American embroidery has reflected the popular tastes of Europe. The culture which linked North America to Europe encouraged a shared embroidery tradition. However, one branch of the textile arts has become widely identified as part of an American cultural tradition: the creation of pieced, applied and quilted covers.

On both sides of the Atlantic, affluent, leisured ladies pieced domestic items such as bedspreads, tablecovers, pelmets, curtains and cushioncovers. This was especially so during the later decades of the nineteenth century when fragments of dress silks and plush furnishing fabrics were used. Two nineteenth-century quilts are illustrated (EG 3432, 2543).

Such fashionable leisure pursuits had their utilitarian counterpart: the working of quilts, covers and hangings for warmth, comfort and privacy, particularly in America where hardship and scarcity often accompanied the colonial and pioneering years. Inevitably such circumstances promoted economy in every aspect of domestic life. Functional textiles were thriftily stitched from

salvaged and pieced fragments of worn-out clothes and furnishings. With necessity as a spur to production, speedy techniques and simple patterns were most popular. Straight edges being the simplest to stitch together, simple geometric shapes became the basic unit of composition. In strictly everyday quilts the shapes could be simple squares or rectangles cut from available material such as sacks and provision bags or heavy clothing. Not too many purely functional quilts survive, as these presumably were used until they fell apart, or were recycled into new covers. For greater aesthetic appeal, but still with an eye to speed, several units could be pieced to form a block and many blocks united in a finished quilt top. Many nineteenth-century quilts have block tops (made from pieced blocks). Their popularity may have arisen from the convenience of the technique for busy women: the individual blocks can be worked in the lap, easily transported, and when finished require only a small storage space. Historians (Weismann and Lavitt) have observed that the popularity in America of block quilts began in the early decades of the nineteenth

Boxes, Canadian, nineteenth century.
Birchbark, embroidered with dyed moosehair. Colours include blue, green, red, pink, orange, yellow, brown and white. The moosehairs are worked in long and short, satin and stem stitches through the birchbark ground. The strawberries on the cigarcase, flowers on the case lid and on the circular boxlid appear to be worked in French knots. The designs on these two items reflect European styles. The lid of the oval box is embroidered with a scene depicting an Indian, carrying a rifle, amongst plants. Each box has its edge decorated with bundles of white hairs couched by brown linen threads. An inscription in ink on the base of the circular box reads 'Dyed moose Deer, on *birch* bark. Made by Nuns of the Ursuline Convent at Quebec 100 years old *now* June 1883'. The cigarcase carries a label inscribed 'Given to Her Majesty The Queen Mexico'
Oval box: EG 4322, 4.5 × 9 × 3.5cm (1¾ × 3½ × 1½in)
Round box: EG 4418, 9cm (3½in) diameter, 4.5cm (1¾in) high
Cigarcase: EG 39, 15 × 7cm (6 × 2¾in). Given by Queen Mary
(Photograph: Peter Williams)

century, when quilters gradually moved away from the earlier framed or medallion design popular on both sides of the Atlantic. The latter format usually absorbs larger sections of fabric than block quilts, which makes them less economical of fabric and workspace.

Traditionally, the basic methods of uniting the three layers comprising a quilt are by intersecting straight lines of stitches which penetrate all layers, or by a series of individual, evenly spaced knots or ties through the three sections.

As privations eased, the need for strictly useful quilts lessened. The selection of materials to be pieced and applied, the design content of the quilt top and the pattern of the unifying quilting stitches increased in importance over functional value.

An extensive range of quilt patterns and names testifies to the creativity and enthusiasm of the quilters, boosted when the need for economy diminished. The once-frugal piecing techniques retained their popularity, but patterns and methods relying on larger lengths of increasingly available fabrics were also used. Appliqué quilts are commonly regarded as typically American,

although the technique and the motifs used also appear in British traditional quilts. Quilters of the Pennsylvanian Amish communities prohibited by religious laws from using decorative patterns were enthusiastic consumers of fabrics in intense and jewel-bright colours. Large blocks and strips of vibrant materials were joined to form quilt tops which no one could call plain.

When living conditions and quality of life improved, American quilters continued to follow their craft. The quilting group or 'bee' was a focal point of social activity in many small and isolated communities. A gathering ostensibly to undertake useful work could also provide an opportunity for companionship and jollity: surely one reason for the tenacity of quilting in rural areas. The mid-twentieth-century interest in quilts and quilters revealed how hugely important these textiles were in many women's lives. Choosing materials, planning and executing a design provided an opportunity for creative expression which would otherwise almost certainly have been denied them. Today, humble and extravagant quilts are preserved as albums of historic textiles and indirect records of events in America's pioneering past.

CHAPTER 3

EASTERN MEDITERRANEAN TREASURES

Turkey, Greece and Persia

Marianne Ellis and Barbara Rowney

THE EASTERN MEDITERRANEAN embroideries in the Collection are unique in that about one-tenth of them were given by one person. Her name was Essie Newberry and she gave some forty-five pieces that originated in the countries now called Turkey, Greece and Iran. Mrs Percy Newberry, as she was usually known, was a founder member of the Guild and a great friend of its President, Miss Louisa Pesel, who was an authority on Greek embroidery. Together they wrote an article for *A Book of Old Embroidery* by A. F. Kendrick, in which they expressed their hope that people would examine their own treasures and in doing so would increase their knowledge and help to revive the craft of embroidery. Presumably it was to provide examples for those without private collections to study and enjoy that Mrs Newberry gave so generously to the Guild. Three items that were illustrated in the Kendrick book are now at Hampton Court; one is a pillowcover from Crete, another is described as a Turkish towel, and the last is a border.

Over the years the pieces from this part of the Collection have been displayed in exhibitions, used to illustrate books and articles in journals such as *Embroidery* and *Embroideress*, and some of them have been loaned to members to study. They are reminders of a past way of life in distant lands, of painstaking techniques and costumes long discarded. Not all these pieces are complete and some are faded and worn but, like so many of the treasures of the Collection, they were given by embroiderers to interest and inspire other embroiderers and in this they succeed admirably.

TURKEY

Mrs Newberry gave the Guild some fine examples of Turkish towels. This is the term generally used to describe the smaller rectangular or square embroideries worked in coloured silks, often with metal threads, on cream-coloured fabric. They were used as towels and napkins, sashes, headkerchiefs, scarves, handkerchiefs, wrappers for presents and covers. Since they were pretty and colourful they were also used as decorations for rooms at times of celebration such as weddings. Great numbers of these Turkish towels were made to satisfy the requirements of the Ottoman household. Several travellers from England from the early eighteenth century onwards have described the beauty of the hand-towels and napkins offered them when they dined in the women's quarters of rich families. The custom was for a servant to come round and pour water, which was often lightly perfumed with rose or orange blossom, over the hands of the guests, and offer towels. Napkins would be used when sitting at the round low tables and then, after the meal, the guests left the table to go through the hand-washing ceremony again.

In her book *City of the Sultans and the Domestic Manners of the Turks in 1836* Julia Pardoe actually mentions the size of the napkins used at one particular meal as being 'two yards' (183cm) long. However there is no standard length for these napkins or towels, and not even one that might be called average. They vary tremendously and the Guild's examples are no exception as they too range from 72cm (2ft 4in) to 188cm (6ft 1in). Towels can be very long indeed; one measures 392cm (12ft 10in), which would fit the description given by Mrs Ramsay in her book *Everyday Life in Turkey* published in 1897 where she explains that a 'narrow napkin which was many yards in length and with finely embroidered borders' was laid on the knees of the twelve diners gathered around a tray of food. This metal tray was nearly a metre (3ft) in diameter and rested upon a stool. It was only possible for so large a number of diners to gather round because they sat Turkish fashion with the right knee raised and the other laid on the floor. The widths are not so variable, ranging from 42cm (1ft 4in) to 57cm (1ft 10in), and many are about 50cm (1ft 8in), the long-accustomed width for hand-woven linen cloth. Pieces that are narrower are usually not for use as towels or napkins, which is one clue to identifying the waistbands and sashes.

The rectangular embroideries do not divide into neat categories. They were used variously as towels, napkins, scarves and covers. The Turkish words used to describe them are *peshkir*, *makrama* and *yaglik*.

DESIGNS

Mrs Ramsay mentioned that the borders of the napkins were finely embroidered but gave no further details. The designs were probably floral for the Turks love flowers and have portrayed them in their textile and ceramic patterns over many centuries. Along napkin borders flower motifs are arranged in repeating patterns. The motifs often consist of a curved stem from which spring flowers, buds and leaves. They can be comparatively simple like the design of a flower and two leaves on EG 3601, or a little masterpiece of design as on EG 4973 with its detail of a pot of flowers encircled by a curved leaf. On EG 4937 a reversed S-spray of delicate gilt foliage frames one flower; this graceful design is often seen on the more delicate towels, sometimes placed so that the flower is upright and sometimes on its side. Another very attractive arrangement is the flowing border seen on towel EG 4380: the design is a repeating one but this is not very obvious because it is 30cm (1ft) long and the short lengths of curved stem give a feeling of movement. The exact opposite feeling is given by towel EG 2355 with its straight horizontal stems and rigid little sprays. These last two towels are examples of two different kinds of design and embroidery. On the former towel the design would have been marked on the fabric first and then worked, whereas the geometric design on the latter would have been taken from a sampler and is more likely to have been worked in the home.

The designs were by no means all floral; fruit such as pears, grapes, melons and pomegranates were popular too. On the towel EG 2254 pears have been arranged to form pyramids on shallow bowls in typically Turkish fashion, reminiscent of the early-eighteenth-century decoration on the walls of the Fruit Room in the Harem at

(*previous page*)

END OF a Turkish nineteenth-century girdle (*uchkur*) placed over a sash end (*kushak*).
The linen girdle or drawstring for trousers is embroidered with two, large, curved, floral-spray motifs in coloured silks in double running, double darning on the diagonal, and *mushabak* stitches and silver-gilt metal thread in fishbone and satin stitches. The girdle was tied to display the colourful embroidery
EG 3631, 162 × 22cm (5ft 3in × 8½in). Given by Mrs Newberry

THE PRETTY nineteenth-century sash of fine cotton has a charming design of cornucopias holding floral bouquets. There are also small single roses and an attractive border embroidered in fine double darning stitch in coloured silks, satin and darning stitches in silver-gilt metal thread, and satin and counted satin stitch in metal strip (plate) from a professional workshop
EG 2649, 224 × 36cm (7ft 3½in × 1ft 2in). Given by Mrs Newberry

Topkapi Palace. (This room is sometimes known as the Dining-room but it was not the custom to reserve one particular room for this purpose.) Subjects such as trees, kiosks, small mosques, rows of arches, tents, Arabic inscriptions, even daggers and parrots, all feature on these embroideries. There are also designs akin to scenic views: some show *yalis*, the pretty wooden summer waterside mansions of the rich beside the Bosphorus, with little boats and birds flying overhead, and others have views of houses, kiosks, trees, gardens and ornamental pools all set on hills. The inspiration for this second kind of scenic design may have been the wallpaintings popular in houses in the nineteenth century.

It is difficult to date Turkish towels precisely but, in general, the ones in the Collection are either from the late eighteenth century or the nineteenth century, or later. There are kerchiefs in Sweden known to be eighteenth-century Turkish work; the designs are of scrolling borders of stems, flowers and leaves, treated in a fairly naturalistic way, the corners filled with pretty arrangements of flowers that sometimes include vases. The European influence is quite marked and shading has been introduced on the flower petals. In the nineteenth century the choice of motifs became much wider than before and some of the work became coarse.

The pattern of two cornucopias holding bunches of flowers, EG 3 1990, is one that has been seen in other collections and in the salerooms. However, even though the outlines of the design – of three roses in one horn and thirteen blue flowers in the other – are the same as on other towels, the stitches are not and the scrolling patterns on the small borders of the towel differ considerably.

These small borders found on many of the towels can be enchanting and often echo the main design. On EG 3601 there are miniature sprigs put close together to make a border and on EG 3603, a tiny scrolling border. These two towels are probably 'city' embroideries from Istanbul as they resemble the one so described in Ayten Sürür's book. These were made in professional workshops and were of a high standard. The best were those produced for the palace and doubtless they were then copied. Distinguishing between work done by professional and amateur embroiderers is extremely difficult in the case of Turkish towels and this includes the sashes, scarves, handkerchiefs, waistbands and trouser panels. Girls embroidered at home for their trousseaus and the ladies of the harem also did fine work. After visiting the Harem of the Minister of Foreign Affairs, Julia Pardoe wrote how one of the slaves 'carried upon a salver a pile of embroidered handkerchiefs, worked by the fair fingers of the two younger *hanoum*s [wives], with gold thread and

coloured silks'. She was told that the flower designs carried messages, like the language of flowers beloved by the Victorians. The same materials were used both by the amateur and the professional with stitches that were not difficult, being variations of darning and double running.

MATERIALS AND TECHNIQUES

Embroidery was worked on hand-woven linen or cotton or a mixture of both. The fabric could be very fine or quite coarse; and even in the Guild's comparatively small number of pieces, the thread count varies between the sixteen warp threads to the centimetre (⅖in) measured on towel EG 3605 and the twenty-one threads on towel EG 15. The latter towel is so fine that it is almost transparent. In some instances thicker threads were added, either in stripes or in patterns. Silk warp threads were sometimes placed at the edges too. For the embroiderer, perhaps the most important feature of the ground fabric is the open quality of the weave.

The most common stitches were variations of darning and double running so it was important to be able to poke the needle easily between the threads. For pulled-threadwork too, a loose weave was essential so that the threads could be wrapped together to form areas of openwork. The threads used were of loosely twisted silk which were produced in Turkey and dyed with natural dyes such as indigo and madder. The chemical dyes developed in the mid-nineteenth century in Europe came to Turkey rather later, so a towel from the late nineteenth century may well be embroidered in silk dyed with natural dyes. Metal threads were much used to decorate these embroideries from at least the eighteenth century onwards. Even in the early-sixteenth-century handkerchiefs, preserved in the Topkapi Palace Museum collection in Istanbul, glitter with little pieces of gold strip that have been pushed through the linen and pressed flat in knots. The metal thread most commonly used later consists of a core of silk around which thin silver or silver-gilt strip has been wound. The core is white if the strip is silver, or yellow if the strip is silver gilt. This thread was used in the needle in the normal way. Thicker metal strip on its own was used to such an extent on the later embroideries that the work can look tawdry.

BATH TOWELS

Metal strip (plate) was used even for embroidering bath towels, as can be seen on the end of one of these, EG 2345. It has been taken right through the fabric to work the stems in padded satin stitch and the flower centres in a counted satin-stitch pattern. This stitching right through the ground fabric with metal threads and strip seems to

(*from the top downwards*)

TWO TOWEL BORDERS of almost transparent fine cotton have been stitched together with an added central band of gold thread embroidery. The floral S-curved motifs are lavishly embroidered with silver-gilt thread and metal strip (plate) in satin and fishbone stitches; petals and leaves are worked with coloured silks in double running and darning stitches. The use of metal thread and strip, in particular, is a feature of Turkish embroidery. On this example the embroiderer has raised the edges of the flower petals with a padding of thread under the metal strip and fashioned an intricate edging of rows of buttonhole stitch worked over lines of metal strip
EG 4937, 25 × 53cm (9¾in × 1ft 8½in). Given by Miss Beale

ONE END of a fine cotton towel with a pretty floral border delicately embroidered in double running and double darning stitches in coloured silks. The double darning is exceptionally fine and shaded on the petals of the poppies which adds life to the work. All the stems have been defined in metal strip (plate) including a small border of tiny buds
EG 4380, 19 × 50cm (7½in × 1ft 7½in). Given by Mrs A. M. Johnstone

LINEN TOWEL end woven with a striped pattern in a thicker cotton yarn. Fruit arranged in a bowl was a popular subject for Turkish towel motifs. The pears are embroidered in *mushabak*, a pulledwork stitch, and with fishbone stitch in silver-gilt metal thread for the centres and outlines. The leaves and bowls are worked in double darning in silk and outlined in metal thread
EG 2254, 144 × 49cm (4ft 8in × 1ft 7in). Given by the NDS

COTTON TOWEL end with a border of blue flowers embroidered in variations of double running stitches in blue silk, silver-gilt and silver threads. This is a fine example of reversible stitchery worked by counting the threads and is probably domestic rather than professional embroidery
EG 2355, 120 × 57cm (3ft 11in × 1ft 8¼in). Given by Mrs Newberry

BORDER depicting vases of flowers encircled by curved serrated leaves worked in double running, double darning and fishbone stitches in coloured silks and silver-gilt thread. It has an uncut fringe beneath a line of counted satin stitch worked alternately in silk and metal threads
EG 4973, 130 × 47cm (4ft 2¾in × 1ft 6¼in)

TOWEL END of fine cotton with large yellow blossoms embroidered in double running and double darning stitches in coloured silks and in padded satin stitch in metal strip (plate) for the stems and stalks. The motifs of the small border echo those of the main design and the towel edge is decorated with a variation of knot stitch in silver-gilt thread
EG 3601, 100 × 47cm (3ft 3in × 1ft 6¼in). Given by Mrs Newberry

(*right*)

SELECTION OF NINETEENTH-century Turkish towels showing the great variety of different designs.
(*from the top downwards*)
BORDER from a linen towel with a vertical chevron design worked in reversible counted stitches in coloured silks and silver-gilt thread. Above are small floral motifs worked with eyelets and variations of double running stitch in coloured silks and silver-gilt thread
EG 3605, 72 × 42cm (2ft 4in × 1ft 4½in). Given by Mrs Newberry

THIS LINEN TOWEL end has been embroidered in silk with pink flowers set against a green openwork (*mushabak*) background using variations of double running

stitches and lines of satin stitch in silver-gilt thread. Spots of metal strip (plate) add further decoration and the bottom edge has been finished with buttonhole stitch
EG 5834, 25 × 48cm (9¾ × 1ft 6¾in). Given by Miss Demetriadi

BORDER of a linen towel woven with a pattern of horizontal cotton stripes and embroidered with small vases holding flowers worked in coloured silks and silver-gilt thread in double running, double darning, satin and fishbone stitches and the warp ends twisted and knotted to form a fringe
EG 171, 70 × 48cm (2ft ¾in × 1ft 6¾in). Given by Mrs Gunning

TOWEL END of very fine cotton with a floral border featuring tulips alternating with other flowers embroidered in small double running and double darning stitches in coloured silks and satin and fishbone stitches in silver-gilt and silver thread. Silver-gilt thread has been double darned in a rich gold band and used to work an edging of two rows of spaced buttonhole stitch
EG 15, 109 × 55cm (3ft 6½in × 1ft 9½in). Given by Mrs Newberry

BORDER of a cotton towel embroidered with a repeating design of a single flower head in shades of blue and green silk using double running and double darning stitches and in satin and fishbone stitch in silver-gilt thread. The edge has been rolled and sewn with buttonhole stitch beneath a small scrolling border of blue buds. Professional work, probably from Istanbul
EG 3603, 120 × 52cm (3ft 10¾in × 1ft 8¼in). Given by Mrs Newberry

TOWEL END of fine cotton richly embroidered with a design of cornucopias holding bouquets of roses and blue flowers. The coloured-silk double running and darning stitches are very fine and both silver gilt and metal strip (plate) have been used in darning and satin stitches. This towel is from a professional workshop; similar designs have been seen on other towels
EG 3 1990, 162 × 54cm (5ft 3in × 1ft 9in)

EMBROIDERED ENDS from two Turkish linen bath towels, nineteenth century.

THE EMBROIDERED ENDS of the top towel have been cut and rejoined side by side. Alternate bands of plain and looped weave indicate that this was a bath towel. Double running and double darning stitches in coloured silks together with fishbone and satin stitches in silver-gilt thread have been used to create these charming kiosks surrounded by flowers and trees

EG 5016, 82 × 91cm (2ft 8in × 2ft 11½in) (single width). Given by Miss Beale

THE LOWER BORDER is from a bath towel embroidered in double darning stitches in coloured silks and double darning in silver-gilt thread. The piece is richly decorated with much glittering metal strip (plate) worked in counted and padded satin stitch

EG 2345, border 48 × 76cm (1ft 6¾in × 2ft 5½in). Given by Dr I. Gough

have been a purely Turkish practice. Metal threads are usually secured to the top surface of the fabric with another thread. The Turks did use couching techniques where they were appropriate, but not on the Turkish towels where the embroidery was required to be completely reversible.

The other bath towel in the Collection, EG 5016, is a complete one of the kind called *havlu* which have a large central area of looped weave and headings of about 26cm (10in) deep left plain for embroidery. There are both narrow and broad bands of the looped weave between the embroidery and the main part of this towel.

These towels are dated to the first half of the nineteenth century by Burton Yost Berry (see Bibliography). He was an American who was in the diplomatic service in the Near East and made an exhaustive study of Turkish towels in the 1920s and 1930s. He wrote that he had seen four dated bath towels with looped weave that were made between 1820 and 1855. However, Pietro della Valle writing in the seventeenth century mentioned a special type of cloth, produced in Salonika, which was woven with a pile on one side and a long nap on the other. This was used for large and small towels and other items he describes as being like open jackets with loose sleeves to put on after bathing. It seems the towels examined by Yost Berry represented part of a long-established tradition of looped weaving.

The nineteenth century saw the introduction of Turkish towelling to England. The idea was copied by the firm of W. M. Christy and Sons of Manchester, a firm of hatters suffering from the effects of diminished trade. Henry Christy brought a piece of the towelling home from Constantinople (Istanbul) around 1840 and copied the looped-weave cloth by machine so successfully that the firm exhibited their new 'Turkish towels' at the Great Exhibition in 1851.

The *havlu* (bath towel) is quite large, usually about 74cm (2½ft) to 91cm (3ft) wide and 168cm (5½ft) long. The colours on EG 5016 have faded, but it must once have been highly decorative with its charming composite motif of a rose and two buds, small tree and little building all framed in gold. More sprays of flowers and trees surround the gold pillars and spring from the curved arches which meet under a little crescent. The whole motif is supported by a fluted basin with curved handles. This design is described in *Ten Thousand Turkish Motifs* by Azak and Koyas as being 'local embroidery from Izmir' and can be seen on a bath towel illustrated in *Işlemeler: Ottoman Domestic Embroideries* by Black and Loveless. Slight differences can be found in the interpretation of the designs: the basins on the towel at the Guild appear to be filled with water! Unfortunately, the photograph in *Işlemeler* does not show whether the towel also has the border of tiny trees, buildings and roses found on the Guild's example. This work on the towels is almost certainly professional and would have been done in a rectangular frame. Whether the designs were stamped or drawn on to the fabric remains a matter for conjecture but it would have been perfectly possible to trace the outlines through the fabric.

Both large and small towels were taken in quantity to the *hammam* or public baths. Some private houses did have their own baths but the visit to the *hammam* was a highly social occasion. The Turkish women had little freedom of movement outside the home, so this was their opportunity to meet others and exchange news. They would spend all day there washing, eating, sleeping and even doing their embroidery. They rested after bathing wearing the towels rather like bath wraps and used headscarves of embroidered muslin to cover their wet hair. It was at the *hammam* that mothers selected future daughters-in-law. Doubtless mothers made sure their girls did not lack for fine embroidered towels. Certain ceremonies also took place at the baths. If the wedding ceremonies lasted for the customary week then Tuesday was the traditional day for the bridal bath when embroidered towels would be displayed. There were also the celebrations that took place forty days after the arrival of a baby when the child was ritually washed. On both these occasions the embroidered towel assumed the importance of a status symbol.

In the home, embroidered cloths were sometimes used purely for decoration, especially on occasions such as the circumcision ceremony when the boy's bed was made very splendid indeed. In the Museum of Turkish and Islamic Antiquities at Bursa there is an example of a bed where many towels, napkins and sashes have been rolled and then looped through each other to form a glittering lattice of embroidery. The lattice rises from the bedposts to the ceiling to make arches over the bed. Weddings too called for ornate arrangements of embroideries. The bridal chamber received special attention according to Fanny Blunt in her book *The People of Turkey* published in 1878. The wedding guests adorned the bridal chamber by covering the walls with rows of embroidered clothes and textiles and above these they hung the smaller towels and scarves and kerchiefs. She wrote that 'this promiscuous exhibition of silk gauze and various stuffs, intermingled with embroidery in variegated silks, gold, and silver, is most striking in effect'. Of course this was for a special occasion but it was normal to use embroideries as pretty and useful covers for all kinds of objects ranging from a Koran to a turban, for money, for letters and for presents.

BOHCHLAR

The larger square cloths, which were used for wrapping clothes, were called *bohchlar*. Such wrappers were very necessary since they substituted for chests. They generally measure from about 80cm (2½ft) to 120cm (4ft) square and were made of two widths of material, either silk or linen, sewn together. In use, they were sometimes folded envelope fashion showing the decorative effect of the border. The cream-coloured background of EG 631 has been embroidered with the stitch known as surface darning on the diagonal, which was much used to work the large covers and hangings as early as the seventeenth century. Their designs followed the ones used for the woven silks with their bold, stylised floral patterns. The Guild has a fragment (EG 4192), not illustrated, of one of these early covers which dates from the sixteenth or seventeenth century. The ogival lattice encloses stylised foliage in the shape of an artichoke or pomegranate, which in turn surrounds a tulip, and is typical of the period. Like the silks, the colour range is limited but this makes the effect even more striking set against the cream-coloured linen. Unfortunately the black silk has rotted away so this makes this design appear rather unbalanced. There would have been black crowns once

(*above*)

Turkish *BOHCHA* or wrapping cloth, eighteenth century (detail).
This square of gold-coloured satin has been richly embroidered with laid and couched coloured silks and silver-gilt and silver metal threads couched in a basket pattern adding depth and shade to the work. The striking design is of flower sprays placed in rows surrounded by a wavy floral border
EG 5277, full size of cloth 111 × 109cm (3ft 7¼in × 3ft 6½in)

(*right*)

Magnificent Turkish nineteenth-century ceremonial shaving robe with matching towel.
This crimson silk robe and towel have been professionally embroidered in chain stitch in coloured silks and metal thread with motifs depicting buildings and flowers. The dense embroidery around the neck opening is a feature of these traditional garments
EG 3835. Robe 149 × 98cm (4ft 10in × 3ft 2¼in). Towel 64 × 112cm (2ft 1in × 3ft 7¾in). Given by Miss Aubrey Smith

(*above*)

Turkish cushion cover, late eighteenth/early nineteenth century (detail).
The cream silk background has been embroidered with a repeating design illustrating a mosque and minarets in a floral setting with coloured silks and metal thread in tamboured chain stitch
EG 1894, full size of cover 77 × 57cm (2ft 6in × 1ft 10¼in). Given by Miss Leveson Gower

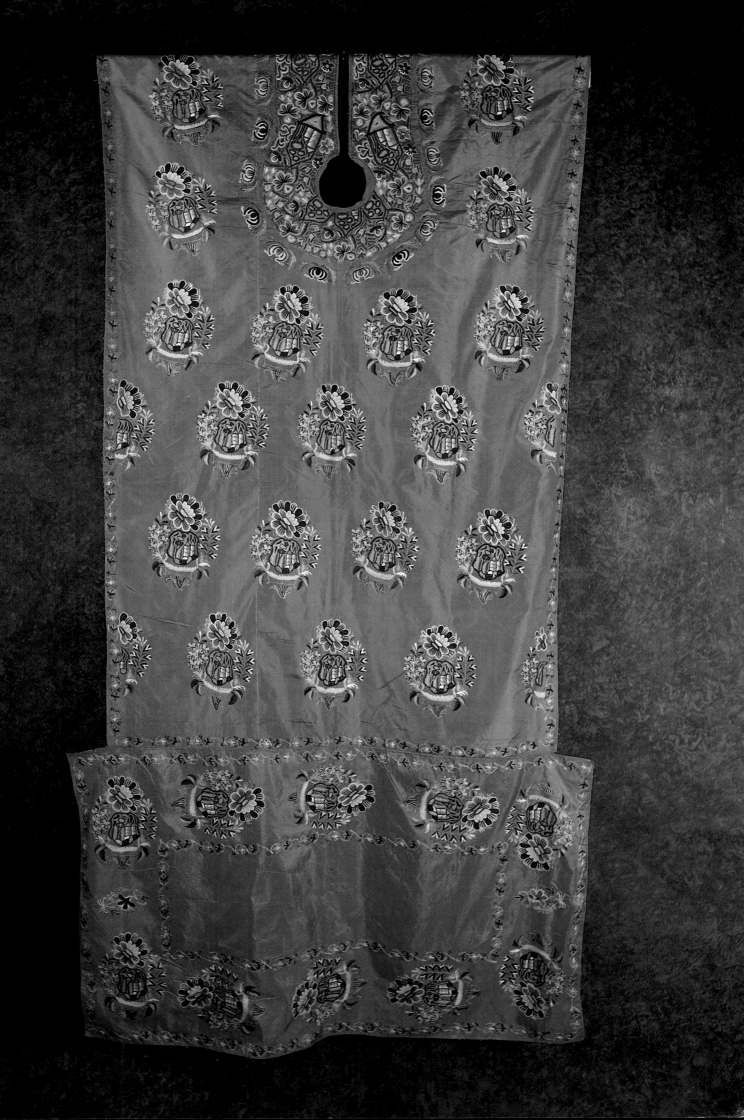

Turkish *bohcha* or wrapping cloth, late eighteenth/early nineteenth century. Square made of two loom widths of fine linen embroidered in surface darning on the diagonal in coloured silks. The stylised carnations and serrated leaves were part of the Turkish design tradition and are often found on darned linen covers and hangings. The work here is comparatively coarse which suggests a late date *EG 631, 95 × 94cm (3ft 1in × 3ft ½in)*

at the intersections and small crescents in the gaps in the curves. The black dots in the little circles grouped in threes are also missing. Decorative motifs based on combinations of three circles and two wavy lines were much used in Ottoman art.

The design on the *bohcha* EG 631 is worked in surface darning on the diagonal which gives quite a faithful reproduction of a twill weave. Here each stitch is worked by taking the needle over six threads, picking up one thread, and moving up one thread every row. This forms little diagonal lines between the silk as seen on the woven textiles. The embroidery did not require much skill and was presumably a substitute for those who could not afford the expensive silk fabrics. The only materials required were a frame, lengths of the fine hand-woven linen and coloured silk thread. In the same way that wool and silk threads can be stitched through linen to imitate a woven tapestry, here silk was darned through linen in imitation of a twill weave. On the earlier embroideries the fabric and stitching would have been finer than on this *bohcha* and the colour range smaller. This kind of design of a composite flower head flanked by serrated leaves is one that was repeated again and again. There was no stigma attached to repeating an old design

(which is why dating the embroideries is very difficult). For instance, the design on the border of a seventeenth-century scarf or towel illustrated in *Turkish Embroidery* by Pauline Johnstone is the same as that on one of the Guild's fragments but the colours and technique of the fragment are different and it is likely it was worked at least a hundred years later if not more. The same design has also been seen on a piece worked in a laid and couched technique, which suggests that this too is a later copy.

The other *bohcha* in the Collection, (EG 5277) is a beautiful silk example. It is sadly worn but must once have been sumptuous. The design is a simple floral repeat which has been worked in two couching methods. Parts of the embroidery have been outlined with gold threads which have now lost their silver-gilt strip. The shapes have been filled with gold threads laid in a basket pattern over padding in contrast to the smoother areas of couched silk threads of white, gold and green. The dark padding of the stems has escaped from the gold thread that was laid across it closely in zigzag fashion. Gold and silver threads often lose their metal strip and the embroideries are left as mere shadows of their former glory.

CUSHION COVERS

Cushions, like *bohchlar*, were a necessity in an Ottoman household. There were no beds as such, but the cushions that served as mattresses, together with pillows, sheets and quilts were taken out of large cupboards to make comfortable sleeping places. There is part of a sheet (EG 3135, not illustrated) of fine striped silk and linen in the Collection that is embroidered quite simply and might have been worked by a girl for her marriage. The pillows or cushions had covers that could be of silk or embroidered muslin.

Many cushions were also needed to make divans comfortable. The divan was a low couch that ran round three sides of the room about 30cm (1ft) from the ground with cushions placed upon it. They were also put on the carpeted floor and Julia Pardoe writes of the girls in Princess Asmé's palace who sat 'clustered together like bees upon their cushions, with their delicate fingers clasped together, and almost making their idleness look graceful!'

More cushions were put beside the *tandour*, a radiator around which the ladies gathered to keep warm. A wooden frame was placed over a copper bowl of charcoal embers and then padded covers were laid over the top of this frame. If it was placed in a corner, then the ladies of higher rank sat on the sofa on two sides while the others would sit on cushions on the remaining two sides. Julia Pardoe declares of the ladies that 'in winter, they have but to nestle under the coverings of the *tandour* or in summer to bury themselves among their cushions, and in five minutes they are in the land of dreams. Indeed, so extraordinarily are they gifted in this respect, that they not infrequently engage their guests to take a nap, with the same sang-froid with which a European lady would invite her friends to take a walk.'

The traditional shape for the Turkish cushion, or *yastik*, is rectangular, similar to that of a bolster. In the nineteenth century the traditional size for these cushion covers was about 125cm (4ft) long and 56cm (2ft) wide. The embroidered ones were made from two pieces of hand-woven linen or cotton which were sewn together to form the covers. This very simple construction has resulted in their often being unpicked and it is easy to confuse the resulting rectangular piece of embroidery with a towel. They were, after all, made from hand-woven fabric of the same width, worked in the same silks and metal threads, and had similar motifs. However, the arrangement of the motifs on the cushion covers usually followed the same pattern, which helps to identify them. The motifs are placed within a wide border with additional smaller motifs in the corners of the inner rectangle. Often lines of scrolling floral patterns outline the wide

border at its inner and outer edges. On the detail of EG 1894 the motifs are composite, consisting of a mosque and two minarets surrounded by flowers above a bowl on which is written '*mashallah*' (what Allah wills). This expression is supposed to avert the 'Evil Eye'. A typical occasion on which it would have been said was when a baby was displayed, as infants were held to be particularly vulnerable.

The embroidery on the cushion cover has been worked with a tambour hook. This embroidery looks like very fine chain stitch on the right side with a thin line of back stitch on the underneath. This can help when trying to identify a piece of Turkish embroidery. Since tambouring produces embroidery that looks different on the front from the back and is not reversible, it was not suitable for the towels, napkins, kerchiefs, sashes, scarves. There is a very beautiful example of tambourwork on part of a cover in the Collection (EG 3630), not illustrated, where roses with many petals, rosebuds and leaves all spring from a graceful, curved stem which is half encircled by a spray of little flowers whose stalk is decorated with a bow of ribbon. The tambouring is carried out in very fine silk and metal thread and is professional work of the highest quality. The contrast between the delicately shaded petals in fine chain stitch and the solid centres of the flowers makes an exquisite piece. Sometimes flower centres are the most delicate part of an embroidery. They are worked with silk thread using a pulled stitch in diagonal rows; the threads of the background fabric are completely covered, thus creating a silk net. The stitch is called *mushabak*, which means netted. This Turkish pulledwork technique using colour is very different from the European work, which commonly uses white thread on white fabric and where the pattern created by the holes is an important factor. Areas of openwork in *mushabak* are a unique feature of Turkish embroidery and add contrasting texture and lightness to the work.

SHAVING ROBES

Besides being used to decorate cushions and covers, tamboured chain stitch was worked on lavishly decorated eighteenth-century shaving robes. Here the flower petals are shaded like the ones mentioned above. The influence of French silk fabrics is thought to have been responsible for the introduction of this change in the designs. Instead of flower shapes being filled with areas of flat colour as found on the earlier embroideries, now shading has been introduced on the petals and leaves. This can be seen on the decoration of the shaving robe EG 3835, but here the work is comparatively coarse, which suggests it dates from the nineteenth century. In fact, it is

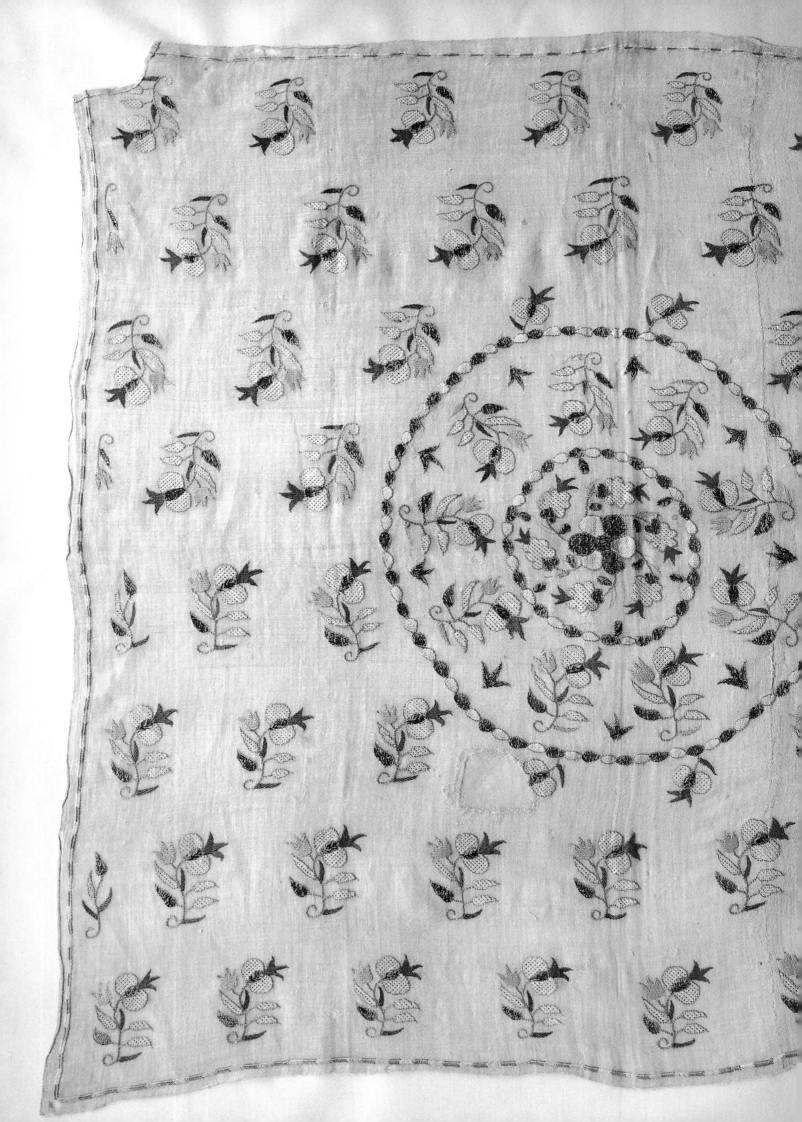

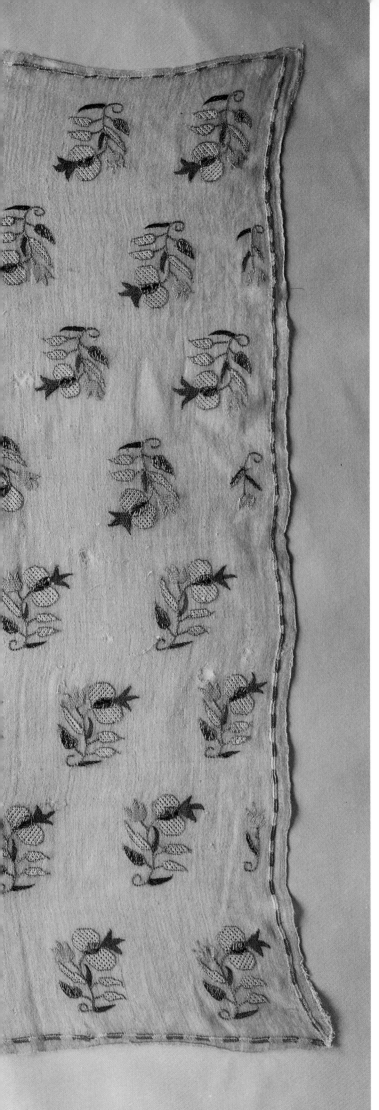

(*above*)

END OF a Turkish nineteenth-century girdle (*uchkur*) with a design based on the 'tree of life'.
Linen embroidered with double running and double darning on the diagonal stitches in coloured silks, fishbone stitch in silver-gilt metal thread, and satin stitch and *tel kirma* in metal strip (plate).
Two girdles were sometimes made from one width of material: here the uncut embroidery has been folded in half to show one girdle end
EG 1170. Two ends embroidered on one width of linen 44 × 45cm (1ft 5in × 1ft 5½in)

(*left*)

EXCEPTIONALLY pretty Turkish turban cover from the late eighteenth or early nineteenth century.
This light, almost transparent, loosely woven cotton cover has been embroidered in coloured silks in double running, double darning on the diagonal, and *murver* stitches and, using silver-gilt metal thread, in fishbone and double darning stitches. A most attractive design of small pomegranate sprays decorates this square and surrounds the small circle in the centre found on all turban covers
EG 2354, 76 × 79cm (2ft 5½in × 2ft 6¾in)

probable that the embroidery worked on this robe was not tamboured at all, but made on one of the chain-stitch machines that reached Turkey in the latter half of the nineteenth century. The evidence for this being that the stitches are comparatively large and very regular and there are many loose ends at the back of the work, whereas tambouring is worked on a frame with the fabric pulled taut so ends are firmly knotted·in.

Even if this shaving robe is a late embroidery, its shape is wholly traditional for it is similar to that of an eighteenth-century one in the Victoria and Albert Museum (illustrated in *Turkish Embroidery* by Pauline Johnstone). The arrangement of the designs is similar too. Around the neck opening is a deep band of embroidery and composite motifs have been arranged alternately in rows all over the rest of the robe. A narrow scrolling border runs round the sides of the garment. Usually a robe and towel were made together as a matching set; here the towel appears to have been sewn on to the bottom edge of the robe. According to the Textile Department of the Topkapi Saray Museum, it was the custom for the bridegroom to have a ceremonial shave before his wedding. Even today this ceremony still takes place. The bridegroom sits in the centre of main square of the town and while the barber shaves him his relations attach money to the robe; the ceremony takes from two to three hours.

TURBAN COVERS

Some of the prettiest embroideries associated with male dress are the turban covers. The turban and robe had been the traditional dress of the Ottoman Turk for centuries until change was enforced by law in 1829. The colour and shape of the turban signified profession or status. Some of them were very large, indeed they were more like hats. Once the long strip of cloth had been wound carefully round the cap, it was left there in position so that both cap and cloth were removed from the head together. They might then have been placed on a turban stand or one of the special brackets that were fixed on the wall to hold the turban. These wooden brackets were themselves very attractive with their rococo curves and carved decoration.

The Guild has four of these delightful covers that were draped over the turbans, EG 2354 (illustrated), 4975, 4976 and 5009. They are more or less square and vary from 79 to 94cm (2½ to 3ft) across. The design usually includes a small central circle, a distinguishing feature helpful when identifying these embroideries. It can be seen on seventeenth-, eighteenth- and nineteenth-century turbans, even though the type and arrangement of the motifs on the rest of the field changed throughout the centuries. In the centre of EG 2354 is a stylised, open flower head of six

petals from which stalks bearing six little blossoms curve out in circular motion. This *charkifelek* motif is one often found on turban covers. It translates into English as 'pinwheel' although the Turkish word has the additional sense of sky and heaven so perhaps 'revolving universe' describes it better. On this particular cover, there is a further circle of rather sedate little pomegranate sprigs surrounding the centre and arranged over the rest of the cover in alternate rows.

Two pieces of fabric were joined together to make the squares before they were embroidered. The seam may or may not come in the centre; it appears that sometimes two selvedges were put together and then the excess material taken from one of the sides. The fabric chosen for EG 2354 was a soft, loosely woven muslin. The little pomegranate sprigs are embroidered in silk and metal thread in a way that is wholly Turkish and enchanting. The centres of the fruits are thickly worked in gold thread in fishbone stitch and surrounded by openwork of white silk. The leaves were double darned, some in gold thread again and some in green. The darning was worked on the diagonal which gives a feeling of movement and growth. This is further enhanced by the way the direction of the darning varies: sometimes it is horizontal and sometimes vertical. The openwork stitch used to embroider the pomegranates is called *mürver*. It is a most intriguing stitch that produces a regular pattern of holes set in alternate rows. Like *mushabak*, the needle goes up and down in rows on the diagonal but the method is not based on faggot stitch. It went through several variations and the present-day versions found in English and Turkish books on needlework are different from the one found on eighteenth-century pieces. This version is somewhere in between the two as the appearance is still very similar both front and back whereas the modern one is not. Flower and fruit motifs on nineteenth-century towels are often worked in *mürver*.

SASHES

Both men and women wore sashes known as *kushak*. Interestingly enough, this is also the term used for the line, often decorated with calligraphy, that runs around the inside of a mosque where the walls and ceiling meet. The *kushak* that went around the person was made in a variety of fabrics and was sometimes embroidered. In the album acquired by the traveller Peter Mundy (now in the British Museum) in the seventeenth century there is a miniature which shows a woman wearing a sash with embroidered ends, holding up the corner of one of her robes to display the patterned facings. By the nineteenth century, the *entari* (robe) had become a gown with deep side slits and long trailing skirts. These too could be tucked up into a girdle for easier walking. At this time the word *kushak* was also used for a narrow shawl that was wound twice round the body and the ends tucked in as a useful place in which to keep such items as money or a handkerchief. In 1845 Charles White wrote that the ladies tucked their embroidered money bags in them. There is a charming small cylindrical bag (EG 3134, not illustrated) in the Collection which might well have been used in this way.

Mrs Newberry gave the Guild a fine *kushak*, EG 2649 (page 71), which is quite wide, 36cm (1ft 2in), and very long, 224cm (7ft 3½in). The design and technique are so similar to some seen in other collections that it must be professional work, possibly from the same workshop. They all have two rows of repeat motifs arranged in threes, with the main design theme echoed in the small borders. In the Guild's example it is a design of flowers and leaves, but had it been an architectural design the border would have been one of tiny buildings, trees and flowers. The floral bouquets have been arranged in cornucopias, and there are also single roses held in ribbon bows. Perhaps the inspiration was a French silk fabric of the kind favoured for the *entari*s. The petals are shaded and worked in very fine double darning called *pesent*. Louisa Pesel included the stitch in her portfolio of *Stitches from Eastern Embroideries*, published in 1913. She worked examples of the stitches which can still be seen in the Textile Study Rooms of the Victoria and Albert Museum.

The term *kushak* seems to have been a fairly general one but the *uchkur* is a much more specific word referring to the drawstring used to hold up the *shalwar* or trousers, worn by men and women. The Guild has several *uchkurlar* although not all are complete articles. The design and stitching of the embroidery ranges from sophisticated professional work to folk-art pieces. They measure from about 21 to 23cm (8 to 9in) wide and from 180 to 200cm (6 to 6½ft) long and on all the Guild's examples the two ends have been embroidered to depth of about 26cm (10in). Some have two selvedges, indicating that the fabric was woven to this narrow width, but quite often two items were made from one length of wider fabric very similar to that used for towels. Sometimes the designs for the two girdles, worked side by side, were the same, and sometimes not. The uncut rectangle with designs embroidered at its ends can easily be mistaken for a long towel or napkin. However the small border at the edge of the embroidery can give a clue. If it is in two parts, ie broken in the middle, to allow for the subsequent division, then the item is two uncut sashes. Just to add further to the confusion, sometimes the two embroidered ends were cut off and then resewn together side by side. The result can easily be mistaken for a towel end.

The bunches of grapes embroidered on the ends of *uchkurlar* symbolise fertility, and were believed to bring wealth, happiness and many children. The 'tree of life' also stands for a large and healthy family and for long life, and was much used to decorate the young bride's trousseau. The large blossoms and upright central stem seen on EG 1170 illustrated is symbolic of the tree of life, even though the tree has become a root from which branches with leaves and flowers spring. The embroidery is competent and reversible and mostly worked in double darning on the diagonal. Here the outlines of the shapes would have been drawn on the fabric, and then the embroiderer would have filled them in with this rather mechanical stitch counted over the threads. Unfortunately metal threads and strip were used to excess as the centuries passed and the heavy stems worked on these embroideries upset the balance of the design.

The double darning worked within the flower shapes on EG 3631 (page 71) is quite different. This embroidery looks professional both in design and workmanship. The motif is beautifully balanced with its S-shaped curve springing up from a leafy coiled stem bearing sprays and flowers and finally arching over a rose with many petals. The silk embroidery is double darned but freely so that it changes direction to suit the lines of the drawing. On EG 3604 (not illustrated) there was no need to trace a design on to the fabric before embroidering the flowers in little vases. These little repeating motifs are the kind found on samplers which were then copied stitch by stitch. The work is very fine and must have taken many hours to complete for it is worked over two threads only. The larger petals have been embroidered in tiny double running stitches carefully arranged so that the diagonal lines radiate from the centre. In contrast, the vases were decorated with openwork in blue silk and have little centres of silver thread. It is tempting to speculate that this *uchkur* was made at home and the design taken from a sampler treasured by the family. Both these fine examples of different reversible techniques were given by Mrs Newberry.

WOMEN'S TROUSERS

The basic items of female dress were trousers (*shalwar*), an undershirt (*gömlek*) and a robe (*entari*); over these a sleeveless jacket or waistcoat called a *yelek* was sometimes worn or perhaps a cloak. The details of shape and length of all these garments changed over the years and, as can be imagined, there are problems in knowing exactly what the women did wear because they were completely muffled up in cloaks and veils when outside the house. When inside the *haremlik*, they only saw the men of the family and female friends: male visitors were

PANELS FROM Turkish women's baggy trousers (*shalwar*). Part of a full-length cotton side panel embroidered with rows of small stylised roses decreasing at the bottom to fit the ankle. The stitches used were different from the ones on Turkish towels because the reverse side of the embroidery would not be seen: they are half cross stitch in coloured silks and surface darning and false satin stitches in silver metal thread
EG 2358. Full size of panel 84 × 42cm (2ft 6¾in × 1ft 4½in)

(*below right*)
PART OF A fine full-length cotton panel delicately embroidered with pretty sprays of flowers in coloured silks and silver-gilt metal thread. Vertical stripes are a feature of *shalwar* panels; these decorative gold ones have been worked in surface darning
EG 2732. Full size of panel 100 × 39cm (3ft 3in × 1ft 3¼in). Given by Mrs Newberry

(*left*)
PART OF A TROUSER PANEL of linen with an all-over design of flowers and leaves in pink, blue and green silk worked in a variation of tent stitch and in false satin stitch in silver-gilt metal thread. The embroidery narrows at the bottom to fit the ankle and is finished with a narrow border of needleweaving
EG 2987. Part of trouser panel 57 × 48cm (1ft 10¼in × 1ft 6¾in). Given by Miss S. Frances

(*above*)

DETAIL OF ONE END of a late-nineteenth-century Turkish scarf or stole.
Organdie scarf with a border design of small cornucopias and scrolling leaves embroidered with satin and stem stitch in both silk and silver-gilt metal thread. The Sultan's *tughra* (monogram), crescent, stars and text were popular motifs worked on embroideries designed for the tourist market
EG 3832. Full size of scarf 255 × 54cm (8ft 3½in × 1ft 9in). Given by Queen Mary

(*left*)

DETAIL OF A TURKISH nineteenth-century kerchief (*chevre*) with charming bird motif.
The designs on these attractive headsquares vary from region to region. The embroidery here is in double running, double darning and *mushabak* stitches in silk and satin and double darning in metal thread. The edges here are finished in Armenian edge stitch but they are often more elaborate
EG 5010, 77 × 80cm (2ft 6in × 2ft 7¼in). Given by Miss Beale

entertained in the men's quarters, the *selamlik*. There is an amusing account by Nicholas de Nicolay of his solution to the problem. He was a Frenchman who went to Constantinople in 1551 to make drawings of costumes. When he realised that it was impossible for him to observe them first hand, he made the acquaintance of a eunuch who had been brought up in the Palace and knew what clothes were worn by the women. This eunuch 'caused to be clothed two publique Turkish women, with very rich apparell', bought from the *bedestan* or bazaar, so that Nicholas could make his drawings.

Levni did not have to go to such lengths before producing his miniatures. He was the court painter to Sultan Ahmed III and recorded the costumes of the palace beauties in detail. At this time, which was about 1725, the trousers were very full and came right over the ankles. In some of the paintings, which are single figure studies, it is possible to see the embroidered ends of the *uchkur* through the undershirts which are almost transparent and reach to the ankle. This fashion eventually changed so that the undershirts were tucked into the trousers and the embroidered *uchkur* ends were even more visible.

There is a description of *shalwar* (trousers), as they were worn in the 1840s, given by Charles White who lived in Constantinople at that time. He reported that they were almost three metres (yards) around the waist and that they were held up by an *uchkur* with rich embroidery at its ends. He added that the trousers were made of various materials. In the Guild Collection there are some side panels from these very wide garments made of cream-coloured linen or cotton and embroidered part way up the legs with motifs in silk and gold threads where the trousers would show below the robe.

Complete trousers are hardly ever to be found as the construction was such that the two embroidered side-panels could easily be separated from the very wide gusset. Each panel is a loom width of about 42cm (1ft 4in), with casing at the top through which the *uchkur* was drawn. At the bottom the embroidery narrows to fit the ankle, ending with a band of embroidery or needleweaving about 30cm (1ft) wide and 2cm (⅔in) deep which does not stretch across the whole loom width. In some examples the corner is stitched back or removed altogether to shape the wide trousers neatly to the ankle. Usually only the embroidered part of the garment has been preserved and this is often mistakenly described as a towel.

There are several features which can help decide if an embroidery is part of a towel or a trouser panel. The most obvious is whether the front and back of the embroidery look the same. There was no point in spending long hours doing reversible stitches such as double darning and double running when only the outside of the panel would be seen. Instead, a favourite method of working the embroidery was to lay a line of thread which was then covered with a row of half cross stitch. Where metal threads have been used, the difference in the embroidery used is even more marked. The gold hardly shows on the reverse of the fabric, when surface darning replaces double darning and false satin stitch is used instead of fishbone. Another clue is the depth of the embroidery which is much greater than on a towel and often measures about 57cm (1ft 10in). The designs are of floral repeat motifs, and if there are vertical lines of needleweaving in white silk the embroidery is almost certainly to have been for a trouser leg. Perhaps the striped effect was popular because it echoed the woven striped *shalwar* materials.

The trouser ends in the Collection vary from the simpler ones made of quite coarse material to an exquisite one, EG 2732, made of fine muslin, given by Mrs Newberry, which surely was for wearing on special occasions. It is beautifully worked with delicate little sprays of flowers and curving foliage arranged closely together in alternate rows. Between the flowers are stripes of gold which must have caught the light when the garment was worn. The effect would have been stunning.

Another particularly interesting piece is EG 2987, originally catalogued as a Turkish towel end. This can be fairly easily identified as part of a trouser leg by the depth of the embroidery and by the little needlewoven band at the bottom which stops short of the edges to allow for the gusset. However, the colouring and, above all, the filling stitch used are different from the rest. It is the variation of tent stitch which Louisa Pesel recorded in her portfolio. She worked out these stitches from the embroideries and the only reference she gives for this particular one is Algeria. Perhaps the girl who did the needlework came from a distant part of the Ottoman empire and preferred to use the stitch she had learnt there.

The little motifs found on the trouser legs are extremely attractive. They are usually floral with an overall repeating design, arranged in different ways such as in stripes or horizontal rows. Only a few colours are used for the embroidery which could be dull, but a lively effect is produced by using gold or silver thread, sometimes both, and by alternating the colour combinations used within the motifs. This happens on the towel borders too where, for instance, a bowl of pink pears is flanked by others containing blue fruit. Sometimes the colours of the flower heads in the scrolling borders alternate in the same fashion. The Turks were very ingenious in the way they invented so many ways of interpreting floral themes and arranged them to suit the particular scale of the different household articles and garments.

SLIPPERS

Some of the goldwork technique which has been used on the pair of red embroidered velvet slippers (EG 4, EG 4a 1990) is called *dival* work; this was much used on elaborate bedcovers, prayer mats and robes in the nineteenth century and is associated with the city of Bursa. Usually five strands of fine silver-gilt wire are taken forward and back across a foundation of pasteboard and the effect is very like a close satin stitch. The embroidery suggests these slippers are from Turkey, but light embroidered slippers were also worn in other parts of the Ottoman empire, notably in Yannena (now in Greece). The Turkish ladies wore light slippers at home in the harem or went barefoot. The equivalent expression for 'pin money' in Turkish is *pashmaklik*, which means 'slipper money', perhaps an indication that embroidered slippers were a favourite purchase made by a Turkish lady. Julia Pardoe visited the Shoe Bazaar in Constantinople and wrote enthusiastically about the colourful display of footwear. She said the slippers were the most beautiful of the shoemakers' wares and were decorated with gold embroidery and jewels. She also explained that if a pair was left at the bottom of the stairs to the harem, this indi-

cated that there was a female visitor within. Apparently even the master of the house would not enter under such circumstances. Prolonged visits did not mean permanent banishment though, as a slave would then be sent in advance to give the ladies due warning of his approach.

HEADSCARVES

Designs with flowers were much used for the headscarves which were an indispensable part of women's costume. Square kerchiefs with printed floral designs are much worn in Turkey today. The old square embroidered ones called *chevre* are quite large and measure from about 80cm (2½ft) square to over 100cm (3¼ft) square, and are all similar in the general arrangement of the designs. This consists of a border that goes all around the edge and a design in each corner that faces towards the centre. There is no embroidery at all in the middle of the square. It would be interesting to know if these *chevreler* are what Julia Pardoe meant when she recounted how she bought from the bazaar 'a couple of richly worked handkerchiefs, used by the ladies of the country for binding up the hair after the bath, which are

RED SILK-VELVET SLIPPERS, probably Turkish, nineteenth century or later. These are lined with silk embroidered with Turkish *dival* work with gold wire and bullion *EG 4 and 4a 1990. Slipper length 27cm (10½in) (Photograph: Embroiderers' Guild)*

PINK SILK JACKET, in the style of the 1860s with Turkish metal-thread embroidery, possibly given to Queen Victoria. The jacket has a flared bodice back, two side fronts without a front fastening, dropped shoulder seams and flared sleeves. It is lined with cotton and has a drawstring at the waist. This sumptuous embroidery has been worked in silver thread, sequins and beads by professional embroiderers
EG 155. Neck to hem 58cm (1ft 10½in). Neck to wrist 97cm (3ft 2in). Hem 188cm (6ft 1¼in). Given by Queen Mary (Photograph: Embroiderers' Guild)

embroidered with a taste and skill truly admirable'. She also described how one of the ladies 'flung a handkerchief over her head, and fastened it under her chin' when a slave announced the gentlemen of the family were coming to the principal apartment.

A particular feature of these headsquares is their prettily decorated edges. These can be worked in a variety of ways such as Armenian edge stitch, buttonhole stitch or in oya needlelace. In the case of EG 2431 (not illustrated), the sides have actually been cut in scallop shapes and then a buttonhole edging added; this was worked using silk and metal threads alternately. Another *chevre* is trimmed with oya worked in silk thread. Oya is a type of knotted lace made with the needle and it is still done by Turkish women today. The most attractive of the

headsquares is EG 5010 (page 87) but, like so many of these delicate Turkish embroideries, the colours have faded, and on the scrolling border design which would once have sparkled with silver, the metal strip has worn away from its white silk core. In each corner is a charming small bird with a little crown on its head perched on top of a stylised bouquet of flowers and green curls of delicate foliage.

Some of the headsquares look as though they were professional work, particularly the ones that have rococo designs of trailing ribbon and loops. They are coarser versions of the delicate eighteenth-century scarves. Both types were worked in double darning but often low-grade metal strip was used on the coarser scarves instead of fine gold and silver threads, which gives a rather clumsy appearance to the embroidery. There are others which are beautifully worked in fine, counted embroidery using variations of double running stitch.

ROYAL GIFTS

Several Eastern Mediterranean items in the Collection came from members of the British royal family, in particular Queen Mary. The most impressive of these royal gifts are a jacket of pink watered silk, EG 155, and two matching skirt lengths. It is thought that they were a present made to Queen Victoria. This seems likely since it had been customary for sumptuous fabrics to be presented by the Sultans from at least the time of Suleyman the Magnificent. Certainly it is known that the British Queen gave a magnificent chandelier to the Sultan's new palace, Dolmabahçe, to which he moved in the middle of the nineteenth century. The cut of the bodice is that of the European fashion of the 1860s and the embroidery is of the highest professional standard, similar to that produced in the Palace workshops. The thread used is silver passing, which is solid silver wire, worked over card shapes in satin stitch to give a raised effect. Little chips of silver purl cluster in the flower centres and the lines of the design are made of silver-linked sequins with single sequins adding extra decoration. The design is more European than Turkish and the embroidery itself is also rather different from the usual Turkish *dival* metal threadwork. To work that technique, metal threads are couched back and forth over card but not taken through the fabric. Here four strands of silver threads are actually sewn right through the background fabric. The effect is magnificent and fit for a queen.

Two pretty scarves, EG 3832 (page 87) and 5024 (not illustrated), made of cotton organdie and embroidered with delicate floral designs were also given by Queen Mary and date from the third quarter of the nineteenth century when large scarves of this type were being produced in professional workshops, probably for the tourist or export market. EG 3832 has the expression '*mashallah*' (what Allah wills) embroidered on it underneath a representation of the Sultan's monogram or *tughra*. The monogram does not imply some connection with the palace but was a decoration added to appeal to Western taste.

Scarves like these would have been on sale in the bazaar when the Prince and Princess of Wales visited Constantinople in 1869. According to W. H. Russell, in his journey called *A Diary in the East during the Tour of the Prince and Princess of Wales 1869*, the royal couple much enjoyed an expedition to the Grand Bazaar in the guise of Mr and Mrs Williams.

> The Prince put on the most humble dress a prince could wear, and the Princess . . . equally contributed to the innocent imposture, which went so far as to arrange that any gentlemen of the suite who might be in the bazaar, was to say, 'How do you do, Mrs Williams?' if they met the party on their rounds.

He goes on to say that the Princess went there twice more; the second time being on the return journey from the Crimea when she escaped from the ship to have 'a last fond look at the Bazaars'.

GREECE

Mrs Newberry gave Greek as well as Turkish embroideries to the Guild Collection. It seems reasonable to suppose that the pieces were acquired in Egypt since her husband, Professor Newberry, was an Egyptologist who worked there from before the turn of the century and was with Howard Carter at the time of the Tutankhamun tomb discoveries in the 1920s. There is an account in *Embroidery* (Vol 4, no 2, 1953) of Mrs Newberry being given the king's shroud to repair but sadly she was then stopped by the authorities. Two photographs of her own work are published in the same article. One is of a cushion with motifs very like those found on Greek island embroideries; perhaps this was the type of embroidery she admired the most. The two floral motifs within squares are very similar to ones worked on a Greek towel that she gave to the Guild along with eleven other Greek pieces. The little trees and sprigs also appear on other Greek island embroideries. The way Mrs Newberry took motifs she liked from another culture and reinterpreted them in her embroidery is much the same process that the Greek islanders used themselves. She has arranged the motifs in an overall design suitable for a cushion and worked them in counted stitches. The result is certainly inspired by Greek island embroidery but could never be mistaken for it. Oddly enough, this design was copied in its entirety in the 1950s by Dorothy Carbonell, a Guild member who admired Mrs Newberry's cushion so much that she proceeded to work it as a rug. Mrs Carbonell also bequeathed some old Turkish and Greek pieces of embroidery to the Guild. Many of these, like the Newberry ones, are fragments but they are full of interest for the embroiderer.

Embroideries from the Greek islands were worked in preparation for a girl's marriage. She was expected to start working them from the age of six and besides those she made herself she might also receive ones that had been passed down the family from mother to daughter. For her house she would need furnishings such as cushion covers, bedspreads, bed valances, pillow covers, napkins and towels, and perhaps bedtents, depending on the customs of the bride's particular island. For her costume, embroidery was generally worked on the sleeves and the skirt borders of the chemise, and on such items as kerchiefs and aprons. The work was carried out in coloured silk threads on hand-woven linen, cotton, or a mixture of both, and the same patterns were used from one generation to another. This makes it virtually impossible to date the embroideries but it is generally assumed that the surviving ones are from the seventeenth to the first half of the nineteenth century.

THE DODECANESE

The spectacular bridal bedtents from the island of Rhodes were commented upon by the French botanist, Pierre Belon, as early as the sixteenth century. He noted that they were worked in cross stitch and were different from Turkish work. The tents from Rhodes were designed to divide off the marriage bed from the rest of the living area of the house. They were bell shaped and constructed of twenty or more panels that tapered towards the top where they hung from a carved wooden roundel. The front and side panels were decorated with embroidery but not the ones at the back, hanging against the wall out of sight. The embroidery on either side of the entrance could be very rich, with additional deep horizontal bands of pattern, and peacocks are often to be found standing guard against evil spirits in the space above the opening. The Guild's two side panels, EG 5389 (detail illustrated), which are joined together, are very typical with their large motifs and simple colour scheme of red and green used alternately. These large Rhodian designs, locally called '*glastra*' or 'flowerpot' patterns, are unique to the Dodecanese. Some of them have a heraldic appearance and have been described as coats-of-arms. It would be fascinating to think they were linked to the armorial bearings on the surcoats of the Knights of St John, who made Rhodes their home for some two centuries after the fall of Acre.

Besides having unique designs, unusual stitchery is found on some of these Rhodian embroideries. It was very densely worked in an exceptionally thick, loosely twisted silk thread on a firm medium-weight linen. Several explanations have been put forward for the plush-like appearance of some of the embroidery. These include using silk with a special twist and raising the stitch by crossing the threads over a small stick which would then have been withdrawn. Another suggestion was that the stitching was done on a loosely woven cloth which was then washed and shrunk thus tightening the fibres round the silk thread. Certainly, different sizes of cross stitch were used depending on the effect required and, in order to get a high relief, more stitches were sometimes worked on top of them. In some places the first diagonal appears to have been laid very loosely and then the second diagonal stitch pulled firmly down; in others, the second diagonal stitch has been laid loosely, giving a higher cross stitch. Some areas in the embroidery are more raised than others, resulting in a changing tone effect due to the variations in tensions and the direction of the stitches.

Not all Rhodian embroidery was of this heavy character though. The Guild has part of a bed valance (not illustrated) which has a particularly attractive design of ewers that resemble elaborate coffeepots. This design is symbolic of the marriage ceremony and is also found on wedding sheets from Epirus, in mainland Greece. Another valance belonging to the Guild, EG 5390, is from Patmos which is also in the Dodecanese, but the embroidery is quite different from that of Rhodes. The embroideries from mainland Greece and the islands are very regional in character, for they were shaped by diverse influences especially those of trade and foreign domination.

The designs on the bed valance from Patmos mentioned above show a combination of two patterns which are found on many Dodecanese embroideries. These are the pattern of leaves arranged in pairs (*platyphylla*) and the design of stylised branches and birds (*spitha*). Here the combined pattern, with its broad leaves in red silk and the branch in green, is arranged alternately, with more broad leaves in cream between. There are also pairs of tiny birds, deer with long antlers and miniature trees. All the embroidery is in fine darning techniques and counted satin stitch which has been beautifully worked with great attention to detail; even the direction of the regular surface darning on the two halves of the broad leaves is deliberately changed so that the depth of colour varies. Sadly this is only a piece of the original valance. It is likely that this is because, once the embroideries were no longer made, many of them were cut up in order that each daughter on her marriage might have her share. It seems that on Patmos whole bedcurtains were embroidered with this charming pattern of broad leaves, branches, small animals and birds. On this island it was the custom to hang a decorative bedcurtain across the front of the bedspace to screen it from the rest of the room. Every inch of the space above the opening of the

DETAIL OF A BEDTENT from the island of Rhodes, probably eighteenth century.

Linen panels are embroidered with bold motifs in thick red and green silk, mainly in cross stitches. Some of the motifs have a heraldic appearance perhaps due to the long association of the island with the Knights of St John *EG 5389. Full length of panel 211cm (6ft 10¼in). Top width 41cm (1ft 4in). Bottom width 94cm (3ft ½in) (Photograph: The Embroiderers' Guild)*

curtain was filled with pairs of embroidered birds, symbolic figures, ships and animals all facing towards the central motifs. The whole effect must have been stupendous.

THE CYCLADES

There is some doubt about the origin of border EG 2723 (illustrated with the valance) embroidered in red silk with geometric patterns. Its hexagon and diamond pattern worked in red surface darning suggests it may come from Milos in the Cyclades.

Many red surface-darned embroideries were also worked on the island of Naxos. The Guild has two examples of these (not illustrated), and one is particularly interesting because it is thought to be an early piece. If so, it could throw some light on the development of the patterns. The geometric all-over patterns ascribed to Naxos

were considered by Professor Wace to be an elaboration of the broad-leaf motif but James Trilling in *Aegean Crossroads* shows how a French sixteenth-century lace pattern may have been their ancestor. The whole subject of the design influences on these embroideries and exactly where they were made is fraught with speculation and uncertainty. Hardly any of the pieces are dated and by the time they attracted the interest of the archaeologists at the British School in Athens they were no longer being made and many had been divided and fallen into the hands of dealers.

The sad fate of costumes was reported by Theodore Bent in his book, *The Cyclades*, published in 1885. He was very interested in the old customs and embroideries and makes several disparaging references to the dealers who had bought up the costumes for their bric-a-brac shops. Fortunately some of the richer families had kept examples which they brought out to show him. He describes how some were still worn on Sundays and

P ART OF A VALANCE from the
island of Patmos, eighteenth
century.
Fine hand-woven linen, beautifully
embroidered in traditional
patterns attributed to this island,
worked in regular surface and
pattern darning, counted satin
stitch, with eyelets in coloured
silks
*EG 5390, fragment 48 × 87cm
(1ft 6¾in × 2ft 10in). Given by
Lady Reigate*

ACROSS THE CORNER, part of a
narrow border possibly from the
Cyclades, eighteenth century.
This type of geometric design
usually associated with the island
of Milos has been finely
embroidered in intricate pattern
darning with red silk
*EG 2723, strip 10.5 × 43cm (4in
× 1ft 4¾in). Given by Mrs
Anstruther*

festive occasions but says that most of them by that date had become curiosities.

Theodore Bent did not write about his travels in the Dodecanese, but he must have found costumes and embroideries there because some belonging to his wife were exhibited at Burlington House in London in 1914. This was the first major exhibition of embroideries from the Greek islands and 192 pieces were displayed including Rhodian tent doors and a complete bridal costume from Astypalaea. Many of the items belonged to Professors Dawkins and Wace who each in turn held the position of the Director of the British School of Archaeology in Athens. Professor Wace, in particular, studied and classified these embroideries and wrote the standard work on the subject *Mediterranean and Near Eastern Embroideries from the Collection of Mrs F. H. Cook*, which was published in 1935. Mrs Newberry and her husband lent some examples from their collection to the 1914 exhibition but these were mostly from Turkey. It would be interesting to know how much she was involved with the exhibition and whether the exhibits attracted much attention. It must have had some effect on the embroidery world because in 1922 Mary Hogarth wrote in *Embroideress* magazine in a review of the first exhibition held by the Guild that there was 'work directly influenced by the embroideries of the Greek Islands'. It would appear that Greek Island embroidery had become fashionable.

COSTUME PIECES

Most of the Greek costume pieces in the Guild's Collection are quite small. Some of them are strips from embroidered chemise borders which were divided up before being offered for sale to tourists. The chemise or *poukamiso* was the foundation of the female costume and was usually made of a white fabric which varied to suit local conditions. In general, the chemise borders were decorated by the women themselves using traditional patterns, the depth of the decoration being decided by the type and length of the garment worn on top. However it is almost impossible to generalise about costume worn on the Greek mainland and islands because it was so regional in character. In fact, styles differed from village to village.

The chemises worn by the women of Attica were called *foundi* or *lazouri* depending on whether they were worked in silk or cotton thread. In her book Linda Welters (see Bibliography) explains that these names were Albanian words and that this area is inhabited by Greeks of Albanian descent. The section of an embroidered hem, EG 3725, is from a *foundi* which would have showed beneath the *sigouni* or sleeveless three-quarter length

jacket. The embroidery is comparatively narrow so that the garment would have been for everyday wear. *Foundi* with deep embroidered bands were worn on a bride's wedding day and thereafter on Sundays and for festivals until she had one or two children or reached her mid-thirties. They chose the designs following the traditions of their village, and either worked the embroidery themselves or called upon the services of professionals. The women of Attica continued making and wearing their costumes until this century. The design on the Guild's hem fragment shows the typical geometric borders surmounted by a band of 'little tongues' (*glossakia*) filled with highly stylised motifs which may have been derived from human figures.

The chemise hem from Arachova, EG 3056, is entirely different. Here the embroidery was worked first and the pieces of the garment were then joined together using elaborate insertions in delicate stitches. The little black spirals are very characteristic of the embroidery designs from this region. The old Arachovan embroidery is renowned in Greece for its excellence; in fact, a form of counted stem stitch is still known as *arachovitiki*.

The third border illustrated, EG 4645, is worked in the types of motif traditionally ascribed to Mytilini which is on the island of Lesbos near the coast of Turkey. Again, these have a character all their own. The border is decorated with rows of little tufted birds, the ones at its edge resting on their beaks and every other one with a crown on its head. Birds wearing crowns fly over extraordinary imaginary spiky little plants to decorate another Mytilini border (not illustrated) in the Collection. The embroiderers must have enjoyed working these amusing little designs which have a quality of fantasy bordering on surrealism.

Chemise hems and sleeves were made into bags for the tourist market. Of the three illustrated, two are made from sleeves from the costume of Attica. The one which is almost completely covered with embroidery, EG 4668, was given by Mrs Newberry and is from a jacket called a *tzakos*. This was a short bodice with a U-shaped neckline that fastened under the bust and had tight elbow-length sleeves. When a girl became engaged she wore one worked with cotton thread like this, smallest, bag. One of the other bags, EG 3641, has red and blue embroidery and is made from a lower sleeve; these sleeves were called *katomanikia* and were just tacked inside the upper sleeves. Their pattern matched the one on the chemise hem. The third bag (in the centre), EG 1294, is worked in black silk and is from a chemise hem from Tanagra in Boeotia. Here the women preferred very dark colours, and black predominated even on their bridal costumes. This pattern is of figures of children, indicating that the chemise was of a type worn for the regional dance.

BAGS MADE in the twentieth century from pieces of earlier Greek costume. (*from the top*).

BAG FROM part of a lower sleeve from Attica, embroidered with red and blue cotton thread in pattern darning
EG 3641. 9 × 23cm (3½ × 9in)

BAG MADE from a chemise hem from Tanagra embroidered with a traditional design of small figures in close rows of tent stitch in thick black silk thread
EG 1294. 25 × 23cm (9¾ × 9in)

BAG MADE from the sleeve of a jacket from Attica embroidered in red and blue cotton thread in straight stitches
EG 4668. 18 × 14cm (7 × 5½in)

Costume was built up from the basic chemise with a variety of over garments depending upon the region. For instance, the bridal costume of Karagouna women from Thessaly includes a chemise, two cotton dresses, a waistcoat, a dickey and an apron of felt. The Guild has some of the embroidered dickeys, called *trahilia*, that were rather like short shirt fronts. They were worn over the chemise both to protect it from the heavy jewellery worn with the festival costumes and for reasons of modesty. The apron or *podia* was decorative rather than functional and, again, it varies enormously from region to region and some costumes do not have one at all. Popi Zora in her book (see Bibliography) writes that in some regions the *podia* had magical powers attributed to it and was often placed over a mother during childbirth. The shape and decoration of the apron can convey the marital status of the wearer. The red apron with the high waist and two gores at the sides, EG 121 1987 (page 100), has the distinctive shape of those worn by women of the Karagouna in Thessaly. It is still worn today, as illustrated in Ioanna Papantoniou's book (see Bibliography). Another type of apron in the Collection is also illustrated in the same publication as part of the costume worn in Desfina in Fokis. However, this type seems to have been worn in several regions this century, including Corinthia, and to have replaced the older ones embroidered by the women

Greek chemise borders, late nineteenth/early twentieth century.
(*from the top*)
Fragment of a chemise hem from Mytilini decorated with small stylised birds embroidered in darning and spaced cross stitches
EG 4645, fragment 12 × 56cm (4¾in × 1ft 10in)

Fragment of a chemise hem from Arachova, embroidered with a highly stylised design possibly based on figures, in double running, double darning and spaced cross stitches in silks and metal thread
EG 3056, fragment 9 × 52cm (3½in × 1ft 10¼in). Given by Miss M. I. Young

Fragment of a chemise hem from Attica, densely embroidered in traditional border designs using tent and satin stitches in silk
EG 3725, fragment 15 × 37cm (6in × 1ft 2½in). Given by Mrs Samuel

(*right*)
Fine red silk breast scarf or *stithopano* from the island of Chios, eighteenth century. This rare scarf is exquisitely embroidered all over with small motifs in coloured silks and silver-gilt thread in double running, counted satin and fishbone stitches with flat, circular tassels decorating its rolled hem
EG 2729, 39 × 40cm (1ft 3¼in × 1ft 3½in)

APRON WORN by women of Karagouna in Thessaly, twentieth century. The apron is made of dark red woollen facecloth cut in the distinctive pattern of this region with a straight central panel, gores on either side and a high waistband of fawn velvet. The garment is embroidered with couched silk cords, silver-gilt and silver metal threads
EG 121, 1987 71 × 45cm (2ft 3¾in × 1ft 5½in). Given by Miss H. Clough

themselves. The aprons are of red felt, with embroidery called *terzitika*. The embroidery is in silk cord and was worked by professional tailors called *terzides* whose speciality was this couched embroidery. The embroidery was often carried out in twisted gold cord and appears on the overdresses of the women's costumes of felt, velvet or woollen cloth and on both women's and men's jackets, as well as on aprons.

Other costume accessories such as scarves and kerchiefs have been given to the Collection. Among these is a very special one, EG 2729, that came from the island of Chios, famous for its silk-weaving industry, and which supplied sumptuous fabrics to the Ottoman empire. This prosperous island, which lay on the trade route between Alexandria and Constantinople, attracted many visitors to its religious and historic sites. They have left behind detailed descriptions and illustrations of the distinctive and unusual garments worn by the inhabitants. One of these is the *stithopano*, literally breast scarf, worn pinned across the bodice of the dress, which was very low cut. According to Philip Argenti (see Bibliography), it was described in 1623 by Heinrich Rantzau as a linen kerchief that covered the bosom. Later, it appears in an engraving depicting a Greek woman from Chios, drawn from life in 1753, in which the pins used to attach it to her costume can clearly be seen. In 1802 a traveller, William Wittman, described in great detail the costumes he saw worn at a religious festival and remarked that 'Some of these females display the upper part of the bosom, which is covered by others with a handkerchief'. However, Philip Argenti states in his book that the majority of the surviving peasant costumes include the *stithopano*. Several examples of the *stithopano* are illustrated in his book but the one of outstanding quality is described as being from Kampos and dated to the early eighteenth century. The Guild's example EG 2729 is so similar that it must come from the same district and be over two hundred and fifty years old. It seems very likely to have once belonged to a noble or aristocratic family that lived in one of the country houses on the Kampos or plain before the massacres of 1822. Details of another very similar scarf have been published in *A Guide to Greek Island Embroidery* by Pauline Johnstone.

All three scarves mentioned are embroidered in fine silk and silver-gilt thread on terracotta-coloured backgrounds. In each case the designs have precisely the same layout, with a small square in the centre of a large octagon, surrounded by embroidered floral sprays. The same spray is repeated four times within the octagon and alternates with a bird, possibly a peacock. The central square has little trees pointing inwards from the corners towards a central stylised flower head. Tiny trees and creatures in rows are worked between the larger motifs to decorate the rest of the kerchief. Small circles of silk and gold threads worked in two rows of detached buttonhole stitch decorate the edges in a distinctive fashion. The Guild's example has been exquisitely worked in minute double running, satin and fishbone stitches to produce a masterpiece covered in tiny embroideries.

Another region, this time on the mainland, that produced many embroideries was Jannina, in Epirus. This was a centre for artists and craftspeople especially under the rule of Ali Pasha in the late eighteenth and early nineteenth centuries. The region exported gold-embroidered garments as far north as Bosnia in the Balkans and to other regions including North Africa. The red jacket EG 4930 is of a later date than this and thought to be of Greek origin. However, the very distinctive cut of its flared sleeves resembles that of jackets worn in Serbia. The embroidery is professional work and beautifully designed to suit the shape of the garment. It has been worked with short lengths of bullion sewn down over padding, seeding and lines of stem stitch. It has neither the special character of the gold cordwork of the Greek *terzides* nor is it the *dival* type of goldwork associated with Turkish embroiderers. Nevertheless it could have been worked in Turkey, but for the moment the precise origin of this treasure of the Collection remains a mystery.

CRETE

In complete contrast to the designs described above, the embroideries from Crete are bold and rhythmic, often with scrolling borders and repeating motifs of vases filled with flowers. All Greek island embroideries have elements that can be traced back to the previous dominant powers of the eastern Mediterranean. Crete however was ruled by the Venetians for a longer period than any of the other islands, from the thirteenth to the seventeenth centuries. During this time, ideas and patterns were introduced and eventually became absorbed into the local Cretan style. The mermaids, birds, small animals and flowers that decorate Cretan embroideries can all be traced back to the patterns on Venetian lace borders.

Much of the surviving embroidery from Crete is from the borders of their very full gathered skirts which were made of five loom widths of cotton and linen material. One type was gathered on to a band under the arms and held in place by shoulder straps, though an illustration in *A Book of Old Embroidery* (by Kendrick, Pesel and Newberry) shows an eighteenth-century dress which has a scoop-neck, front-buttoned bodice to which a full skirt is gathered. Sometimes just the gathered skirt or a decorative border on its own has survived.

SKYROS

Skyros, in the Northern Sporades, was under Turkish rule for many years but this was somewhat mitigated as authority was exercised in conjunction with leading members of the Skyrian population. Elements of Turkish design can be detected in the needlework but, as always with these Greek island pieces, the work developed a character all its own. Floral designs relating to the Ottoman carnation and tulip were popular, as were ships of various types, also birds. Often the embroideries are densely populated with lively little figures, small birds, animals and half-human creatures with large round eyes. Flowers sprout everywhere, from the caps on the little men and the birds' feathers – even the dogs' tails turn into arabesques. The cockerel was also a favourite motif, much used by the women both on household embroideries and on the hems of their chemises, where it appears in miniature.

The Skyrians did not use bedcurtains as the bed was usually situated on a platform at the rear of the house. The bedspreads are the largest and most important domestic pieces, made from three widths of hand-woven linen and embroidered on all four sides. Some of these are decorated with the large exotic ornamental cockerels similar to those found on the piece EG 2843, which has been attributed to the eighteenth century. Certainly the fine

P ART OF A LINEN hanging or
cover with two decorative
cockerels, from the island of
Skyros, eighteenth century.
This piece is worked in coloured
silks in fine embroidery using two
variations of surface darning.
Decorative birds frequently feature
on Skyrian embroidery but these
two fantastic cockerels are the
most magnificent of them all
*EG 2843, fragment 79 × 39cm
(2ft 6¾in × 1ft 3¼in)*

WOMAN'S JACKET, possibly Greek, nineteenth century.
Red facecloth is embroidered with gold metal threads and bullion in a floral design. The garment has three-quarter-length flared sleeves gathered on to a dropped shoulder seam and an attractive scalloped edge finished with gold cord
EG 4930, neck to hem 56cm (1ft 10in). Purchased (Photograph: Embroiderers' Guild)

stitching and subtle use of darning techniques would seem to confirm this date: on the later Skyrian embroideries double darning tends to be used instead of surface darning variations. These handsome birds possibly symbolise fertility and refer to Zeus who was represented as a cockerel on Greek vases. The design of each bird differs in its details especially in the head-dress – one sports frilly fronds and another appears to be wearing a turban. The way the birds perch upon floral boughs and are surrounded by sprouting foliage is reminiscent of sixteenth-century Iznik ceramic plates. It is known that the Skyrians much admired and collected ceramics from other countries so they probably absorbed elements of these designs into their own decorative art.

PERSIA

The embroideries from Persia are extremely fascinating but they raise many questions. Persia, now known as Iran, has had a turbulent history and suffered invasion, political chaos and much destruction. Strictly speaking, this area is western Asia rather than eastern Mediterranean but, historically, Persian textiles and their designs have travelled far beyond its boundaries, and influenced those of other countries. Following the Mongol conquests it was through Iran that Chinese art influenced Ottoman Turkey. Unfortunately, very little Persian work from before the seventeenth century has survived, but there is Marco Polo's report on his journey through Kirman in the thirteenth century which mentions embroidery:

> . . . the women and young persons work with the needle, in embroideries of silk and gold, in a variety of colours and patterns, representing birds and beasts, with other ornamental devices. These are designed for curtains, coverlets and cushions of the sleeping places of the rich; and the work is executed with so much taste and skill as to be an object of admiration.

Later on in the seventeenth century, a Huguenot jeweller called Sir John Chardin recorded his opinion that the Persians 'do all sorts of embroidery very well, especially the Gold and Silver Embroidery'. As to how much embroidery was made during the sixteenth and seventeenth centuries, it is impossible to know, but it was a period when the most beautiful woven silk and velvet textiles brocaded with silver and gold thread were produced, certainly needing no further decoration with embroidery. Similarly, luxurious woven fabrics, such as brocade, were used for household furnishings, cushions, curtains and doorhangings.

FURNISHINGS

The household furnishings in the Guild Collection are mostly covers, used for many different purposes. They fall into characteristic types and are generally the products of professional workshops. The elaborate quilted bedcovers given to Bess of Hardwick by her son following a visit to Persia show how sophisticated that technique had become by the sixteenth century. The Italian traveller, Pietro della Valle, writing in the seventeenth century, refers to quilts being used both as bedcovers and floorcovers and, in particular, to the King sitting on a little quilt outside his tent. The 'tent' was probably like the small painted and gilded pavilions seen in miniatures where the ruler sits on a carpet or small mat.

Examples of fine eighteenth-century prayer mats and bath rugs with floral patterns on white quilted grounds have survived; the former can be recognised by the niche, with a small roundel or panel with inscription, at the apex. They are thought to have been made from the seventeenth century onwards and are particularly interesting because of their contribution to the design features which reappear on the Indo-Persian style developed at the Mughal court and also on the quilts produced by the English professional workshops of the eighteenth century. The Guild has a quilted bath mat from southern Persia EG 240, which has the typical design layout of a central motif with four cusps and four points, with quarters extending out into the field from a triple outside border. On this mat there are stylised flower heads within the medallion and each cusp or point has a small bird or cone (or cypress) on it. The floral sprays arranged on the field and in the border relate to the small flower compositions found on the woven silks. The combination of the coloured embroidery set against a patterned background of fine quilting is very attractive. These mats were used to sit on when dressing after the bath and were placed on a piece of brocade. A woman of the upper class would send her servant ahead to the baths with her mat and other necessary items such as towels and silver-plated copper bowls for pouring water. As in Turkey, the quality of the personal articles taken to the *hammam* reflected the owner's social standing.

The Guild also has another larger, more elaborate quilted mat (not illustrated) which has a similar central medallion and many small flower designs. It is decorated with pairs of small birds, and large and small vases filled with flowers. The top fabric was woven with a cotton warp and silk weft and quilted in yellow silk before being embroidered in chain stitch in bright colours.

Flowers, birds and vases figure too on Resht embroideries. Although this town in north-west Iran, on the Caspian sea, has given its name to this kind of embroidery, Sir John Chardin wrote that he saw it being made in Isfahan by tailors and described it as follows:

> They make carpets, cushions, door hangings, and other felt furniture like garden knots and mosaic work, representing what they please, and all of it so neatly sewed, that you would think the figures are painted though 'tis all of it but patched work; the seam of them is not seen if you look at never so near, they are drawn so curiously fine.

Wallhangings, prayer rugs and saddle blankets were

Q UILTED PERSIAN BATH MAT, nineteenth century. A cotton mat with a central medallion, flower sprigs and a border is embroidered with straight and split stitches in coloured silk. The quilting has been worked in back stitch through cotton wadding. It was customary to use these mats after bathing
EG 240, 93 × 79cm (3ft ¼in × 2ft 7in). Given by Lady Egerton

made using this inlaid technique, which was even employed to make a series of half life-sized portraits of Fath Ali Shah and the ladies of his household. As European influence introduced a new style of furnishing which included tables, sofas and chairs, covers were made for them in Resht embroidery. The large cover in the Guild Collection, EG 596, is unusual because of its circular shape and concentric floral rings. The whole cover is put together from pieces of fabric like an inlaid patchwork. Background strips of closely textured woollen fabric of different sizes have been stitched together and the joins covered with cord. Other pieces of different-coloured cloth in the shapes of flowers and leaves have then been inlaid. Their sharp outlines suggest that shapes made of metal may have been employed to cut them so precisely. After the inlay was completed, chain stitch has been worked with a hook, on top and around them, in coloured silks. No frame was used for Resht embroidery:

the cloth was held in a long clamp that rested on one leg and was held firm under the other. This enabled the worker to achieve the even, white, swirling lines and tiny spirals. The result from a distance is always quite stunning.

Further to the north-west from Resht in the southern Caucasus, between the Caspian and the Black Sea is an area famous for its carpets. It is inhabited by many different tribes and today is divided between Russia and Iran. There is a group of embroideries from this region that have certain similarities to early carpets made in the southern Caucasus and north-west Persia. The ones worked in fine cross or tent stitch have striking patterns in strong colours and were probably made in professional workshops, possibly alongside the carpets they so closely resemble. They are usually described as cushion covers and dated to the eighteenth and nineteenth centuries although some may be earlier. Their layout is symmetrical,

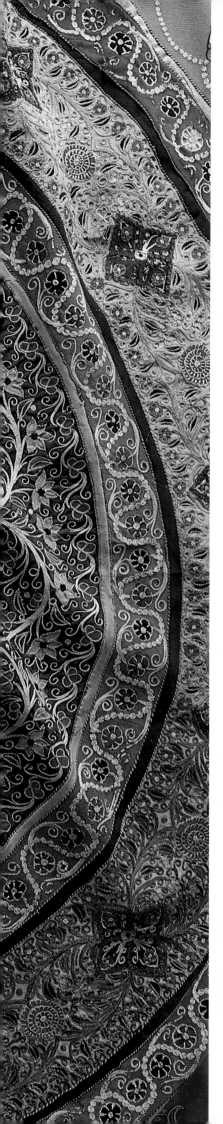

Caucasian/North-West Persian cover, eighteenth century. Cotton ground is embroidered in fine cross stitch using coloured silks
EG 2347, 71 × 43cm (2ft 3¾in × 1ft 4¾in). Given by Mrs Newberry

(left)

Large persian circular cover from Resht, nineteenth century.
Pieces of coloured woollen cloth have been joined and inlaid with many small shapes to form colourful designs, and embroidered in coloured silks with chain stitches using a hook. This is professional work by specialist male embroiderers who continued using traditional techniques
EG 596, diameter 163cm (5ft 3½in). Given by Mrs Stokes

consisting of a large geometric medallion in the centre, such as a star, octagon, or cross, and many geometric floral forms covering the field, which is surrounded on all sides by a small simple border round the edge. The border on an eighteenth-century cushion cover illustrated (Plate 126) in Professor's Wace's book (see Bibliography) is the same as on the Guild's one, EG 2347. The latter has a design of a central octagon with points projecting from the sloping sides. Inside this there are floral shapes including four stylised tulips, and very angular flower sprays with three highly stylised flower heads on either side of them. The dark background and hook shapes seen here on spirals are characteristic of these embroideries. This example has been precisely worked in fine cross stitch and the design carefully laid out in black stitching before work began.

There is another group of embroidered covers with geometric designs from Persia represented in the Collection. These are worked in darning stitches which results in their being considerably softer and lighter than the stiff cross-stitched ones attributed to the southern Caucasus. There is disagreement as to exactly where they were made; some share design elements with the rugs and carpets and others have endlessly repeating geometric patterns. All have narrow single borders and, again, these relate to the carpets but are simpler. Pastel colours are included in the colour schemes and the shapes are outlined in black or dark brown running stitch and upright cross stitch. The shapes are filled with coloured-silk surface darning and set against white backgrounds. The techniques used for these backgrounds vary, which has given rise to speculation that these are domestic embroideries. Perhaps the patterns were put on the cloth by professional designers and the embroidery done at home. The covers are very attractive in the way the darning stitches change direction so that the light plays on the different surfaces and accentuates the shapes of the patterns. Some of the backgrounds are darned in small patterns and some, but not the ones in the Collection, have openwork backgrounds worked in white silk in pulled thread stitches.

Large reversible covers were embroidered in whitework techniques. The patterns are geometric in character and were worked by counting the threads. The embroidery was done on plain cotton fabric with cream or white silk thread and in some instances metal or black thread was also used. The rectangular cover, EG 146 1983, shows how beautifully the designs were planned and worked, with solid satin-stitch patterns contrasting with the openwork which is more lacy in some places than others. The different angles of the silk blocks give a lovely shimmering effect and weight is added to the design by two borders of needleweaving.

COSTUME

Another fine piece of white embroidery, EG 973 (page 112), is part of a quilted cap, and dates from the eighteenth or nineteenth centuries. There is a nineteenth-century complete cap in the Textile Study Room of the Victoria and Albert Museum which is also quilted. Both caps are conical in shape and have designs of birds perching on a small tree or bush. A design based on the same theme has been embroidered in tamboured chain stitch on to another conical cap (not illustrated) in the Guild Collection. Patterns of birds among small flowering branches can be seen on seventeenth- and eighteenth-century textiles, illustrating a romantic theme of Persian poetry where lovers are represented by the nightingale and the rose. The tiny songbirds on the fragment of the cap have been outlined in minute back stitch and their eyes emphasised with fine buttonhole stitch. Their shapes have been padded with blue yarn which throws them into relief against the straight lines of quilted background padded with white yarn.

A rare costume consisting of tunic, headsquare, trousers and bridal shawl (EG 3454, 3459, 3460, 3464) from Persia was given by Lady Evelyn Sykes whose husband was British Consul in Kerman from 1894 to 1901. Whilst Sir Percy Sykes was in Persia, he had as housekeeper his sister Ella who wrote two books about her experiences there. In one of them *Persia and its People* published in 1910, there is a photograph of a woman in an almost identical costume to the one in the Collection. This photograph was helpful in identifying this as a Zoroastrian bridal costume. The figure is wearing a headscarf, a shoulderscarf, a jacket, a tunic reaching below the knees and very baggy, striped trousers. Both the tunic and the trousers correspond to those parts of the costume belonging to the Guild. Their owner would have been one of the few remaining followers of the ancient religion of Zoroastrianism in which light and fire are the most important elements. Possibly the symbols that can be clearly seen on the large bridal shawl refer to these. The inscription says in poetic language that the shawl was a present from a bridegroom to his bride; a translation of this was published in an article about the costume by Mary Krishna in *Embroidery* (Vol 15, No 4, 1964).

Among the best known of the embroideries that travelled to the West from Persia are the women's trouser

PERSIAN WHITEWORK COVER, nineteenth century.
Cotton cover embroidered all over in geometric patterns in cream silk in counted satin and pulledwork stitches with eyelets and needleweaving
EG 146 1983. 84 × 53cm (2ft 8¾in × 1ft 8½in). Given by Mrs C. Wade

(*right*)

ZOROASTRIAN COSTUME of tunic, headsquare and trousers, nineteenth century. Tunic of pieced silk. Front skirt panels embroidered in small *buta* and fish designs in coloured silks worked in small straight stitches. The seams are decorated with a buttonhole stitch variation, the border is decorated with applied strips, couched cords and interlaced stitchery. The round neck is split at the centre back and front and is of cotton. The sleeves are cut in one with the shoulder, the rest of the bodice is pieced silk and the skirt is made of alternately straight and flared panels
EG 3459. Shoulder to hem 107cm (3ft 5¾in). Neck to wrist 73cm (2ft 4½in). Hem width 200cm (6ft 7in)

HEADSQUARE of woven striped silk with a fringe
EG 3461, 87 × 90cm (2ft 10in × 2ft 11in)

TROUSERS. The cotton body of the trousers has been seamed by machine; the lower legs of the trousers are mostly made of joined silk strips backed on to heavy indigo cotton for strength and embroidered in straight, stem and magic chain stitches and couched threads; the inside of of the lower leg is of hand-printed striped cotton. The waist has a drawstring; the lower legs are gathered into a band. Small motifs of fish, circles, *buta*, animals, figures and floral motifs decorate the silk stripes
EG 3454. Length 97cm (3ft 2in). Round each leg 128cm (4ft 2in). Costume given by Lady Evelyn Sykes

ZOROASTRIAN BRIDAL SHAWL, nineteenth century. Dark green silk embroidered in stem, satin and magic chain stitches and couched threads, in coloured silks with coloured paillettes. The large central medallion is densely worked in concentric rows of zigzag stitchery with rings around it of small birds and flowers, paillettes, small fish, an inscription and a circle of large *buta* and front and side views of peacocks
EG 3460, 276 × 92cm (8ft 11½in × 3ft). Given by Lady Evelyn Sykes

Detail of a segment from a Persian conical cap, eighteenth or nineteenth century.
Cotton is quilted in fine back stitch in cream silk with an attractive design of birds and leaves. These motifs have been padded with indigo yarn and the background padded with white yarn. Two segments of the cap were worked flat on one piece of fabric; the top part was then cut and stitched to form half the cone *EG 973. Half of cap 24 × 25cm (9¼ × 9¾in). Given by Mrs Newberry*

pieces often called *nakshe*, which is the Persian word for embroidery or ornament. In the nineteenth century though, they were known at *gilets persans* (Persian waist-coats) because Victorian delicacy preferred not to mention the word trousers. The embroidery was cut from the legs of Persian women's garments, and was very much in vogue for turning into such articles as slippers and waist-coats which, in fact, were often those which the Victorian lady herself embroidered in fine canvaswork. The *nakshe* fragments can be recognised by their patterns which are of floral diagonal stripes. Trousers with such patterns were fashionable as early as the sixteenth century, as can be seen on miniature paintings and on textiles. A sixteenth-century embroidery illustrates a lady fainting with love revealing the bottom of her striped trouser leg.

In the sixteenth century the trousers appear to have been narrow at the ankle but in the eighteenth century they became wider and straight; this fashion continued to the nineteenth century. The patterns embroidered on the trousers followed those of the woven textiles, with diagonal stripes of floral motifs. The embroidery on the Guild's fragment EG 3357 (page 114) is typical, with its two sizes of oblique stripes and the central larger flower motifs surrounded by smaller ones. The fragment is worked in many different colours of silk thread and the whole design was first tacked out in coloured threads before being embroidered in fine tent stitch. The other pieces of *nakshe* (EG 2346, 3360) are simpler in design and technique and, although from different garments, their designs are similar. The black lines of the stripes were worked first and then the motifs and finally the background, in the tent stitch that Louisa Pesel called Algerian. They are both from trouser legs that narrowed at the ankle so an extra piece has been carefully matched and added to make rectangular pieces of embroidery. These two embroideries were given to the Guild by Lady Egerton who was the Russian wife of the British Minister in Athens. It was she who started the Royal Hellenic Schools of Needlework and Laces to which Louisa Pesel was appointed in 1903.

BOKHARA HANGINGS

Among the embroideries which have long been prized by collectors are the covers known as Bokhara hangings (from the name of a district), or *susanis* (needle in Persian), produced in the Central Asian region of Turkestan, now forming part of the modern Soviet Republics of Turkmenistan, Uzbekistan and Tadjikstan. The ancient silk routes passed through this area on the way from China to the Mediterranean. It has had a chequered history, subject in early periods to invasions from the Persians, Turks and Mongolians, and occupied by Russia from the last quarter of the nineteenth century. It is peopled by a wide variety of settled and nomadic groups, mainly Turkic peoples, but also Slavs and Mongolians, and including Christians and Jews. Nine-tenths of the area is desert or mountainous terrain, but it is intersected by fertile river valleys where the main oasis towns of the silk route are situated. The settled populations of these valleys, Tadjiks and Uzbeks, differ considerably in dress and custom from the nomadic desert tribes, which are mainly Kirghiz and Turkoman in origin.

Textile crafts have always played an important part in the economy and culture of the whole region, based upon the production of wool, cotton and silk. Dyeing was also a highly developed art, drawing upon locally available dye substances including indigo (blue), cochineal (pink and plum), madder (orange-reds), and a variety of plants producing yellow dyes. Characteristic techniques of the area are the famous *ikat* silks (the threads pattern dyed before weaving), knotted carpets, and felted textiles made by nomads from unspun wool.

Embroidered items were made by both nomad and town-dwelling women, the large covers, or hangings, being an important element of a bride's dowry. Typically these hangings are decorated with brightly coloured floral motifs worked on a ground which is left plain. The ground is made up of four to six narrow loom widths of cotton, each of which is separately embroidered before being joined. The embroidery is usually worked over inked designs, many of which, it is suggested, were prepared by professional male designers in the towns, a practice which would help to account for the characteristic styles and motifs attributed to particular districts.

Although they are generally known as Bokhara hangings, they were also made in the districts surrounding the towns of Shakhrisyabz, Nurata, Karshi, Samarkand, Khodjend, and Tashkent. All the designs broadly follow a carpet plan, with a border and a field, and often a central medallion. All the motifs are ultimately derived from flower and plant forms; some clearly relate to Ottoman tulips, palmettes and hyacinth sprays, others are more simplified circular flower heads. The motifs are joined by leafy tendrils or spiky stems in repeating patterns.

The most common stitches used are two forms of single-thread couching, in which a continuous thread is used both to lay a stitch and to catch it. In one form, known in English as Romanian couching, the tying stitches are long and loose and appear almost to be twisted around the laid thread. In the second form, known as Bokhara couching, the tying stitches are short, almost at right angles to the laid thread, and worked so as to produce a twill-weave effect across the motif as a whole. Both are stitches which produce solid blocks of coloured silk on the surface of the textile while wasting little of the precious silk on the reverse. All the motifs of these hangings are worked in one or other of these couching stitches, but outlines and stem details are worked in various forms of chain stitch.

The best examples of these bold and beautiful coloured embroideries seem to date from the nineteenth century (see illustrations). Despite the fact that they were principally home-produced dowry textiles, there does appear to have been local trade in the embroideries, which were prized as wallhangings by the urban well-to-do. By the 1870s there was an established demand for them in Russia and Western Europe, a demand which the occupying Russians exploited by setting up workshops employing male Uzbek embroiderers. But, as so often happens, this commercialisation led to a decline in quality. The vibrant natural dyes were replaced by impermanent chemical dyes, and the couching stitches gave way to more easily worked chain stitch, some of which was entirely machine produced. By the 1920s it was reported that the traditional forms of embroidered hanging had all but disappeared.

(*left*)

PERSIAN WOMEN'S TROUSER pieces (*nakshe*), nineteenth century.

(*left*) Cotton embroidered in tent stitch in coloured silk threads with a design of oblique floral stripes *EG 2346, 52 × 40cm (1ft 8¼in × 1ft 3½in). Given by Lady Egerton*

(*centre*) Fine cotton background embroidered with tent stitch in coloured silks with a design of oblique floral stripes. The design of oblique stripes on this fragment closely resembles those on the woven silk textiles *EG 3357, 28 × 25cm (11 × 9¾in)*

(*right*) Cotton embroidered in tent stitch in coloured silks with a design of oblique floral stripes *EG 3360, 56 × 47cm (1ft 10in × 1ft 6¼in). Given by Lady Egerton*

(*left*)

COVER (detail), west Turkestan, Bokhara region, nineteenth century.

Cotton is embroidered with silk, using Romanian and Bokhara couching, chain and open chain stitches. The method of piecing a whole cover from sections of fabric can be seen in this corner area. First, the ground fabric was pieced, and the design drawn on to it. The cover would then be unpicked and the panels distributed amongst several embroiderers. In this border the large embroidered flower heads and leaves continue over the seam joining the sections together, but the technique in the leaves changes between sections from Bokhara to Romanian couching; and the smaller floral/leaf motifs are severed by the seam. That the sections were worked by different people is indicated by these breaks in the design and techniques used. The sections vary in size *EG 5560, 225 × 180cm (7ft 3¾in × 6ft ¼in). Given by Philippa Reeves*

(*right*)

COVER, west Turkestan, Bokhara region, mid-nineteenth to late nineteenth century.

Cotton is embroidered with silk in Romanian and Bokhara couching, chain and open chain stitches. The cover is pieced from seven panels varying in width: the narrowest is 15cm (6in) wide and the widest 30cm (11¾in); the remainder are approximately 28–29cm (11–11¼in) wide. The design incorporates several different types of flowers closely packed and densely embroidered in heavy silks. The hanging is edged with a stitched braid and blanket stitch *EG 2048, 214 × 161cm (6ft 11½in × 5ft 2¾in)*

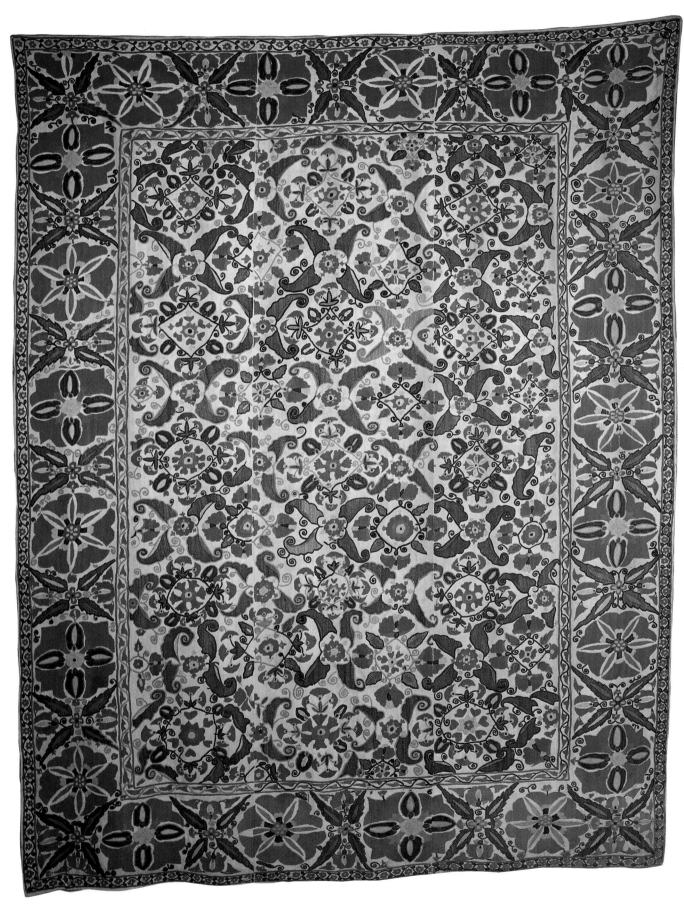

CHAPTER 4

THE INDIAN TRADITION

Court and Rural Styles

Rosemary Ewles

I NDIA HAS ONE of the richest and most ancient textile traditions in the world, encompassing weaving, dyeing, printing, carpet making and embroidery. Despite the decline of private patronage, the loss of export markets, and the importation of Western factory-made goods, many textile hand crafts have survived into this century and are still an integral part of Indian life, whether as a source of livelihood or as domestic work for home and ritual use.

The embroideries of India exhibit a particularly wide range of styles and techniques and have long been a subject of interest and a source of inspiration to Western embroiderers. This is reflected in the Collection of the Embroiderers' Guild, where Indian embroideries have been an important element from its earliest years. It is also one of the few sections of the Collection to which it has been possible to continue to add recent examples of embroidery produced entirely within a folk tradition.

Not surprisingly, most items in the Guild's Indian collection date from the second half of the nineteenth century or from the twentieth century. However, there is also a group of much earlier pieces which reflect something of the style of the Mughal court, and the kind of embroideries produced for the Western market in the seventeenth and eighteenth centuries under the auspices of the East India trading companies.

The provenance of much of the early material acquired by the Guild is not recorded, but it is likely that many pieces were acquired by Guild members, their relatives or friends, during tours of duty under the British Raj. A few have come from missionary contacts, and one piece (EG 202) a detail of which is illustrated on page 126, was given by Queen Mary and was probably originally a gift made to the royal family during a visit to India in the early years of this century.

The Guild Collection includes examples of most of the characteristic historical and regional styles of Indian embroidery, and as such is a valuable study resource for the newcomer to this subject. The only major types of embroidery not represented are items produced for temple or monastic use (which are rare in museum collections in the West), the appliqué work produced in southern India, and the geometric weave-like embroideries of Bihar and Manipur to the north-east.

S HAWL OR SCARF, India, second half of the nineteenth century. The black shawlcloth is from Kashmir, the embroidery professionally worked in Delhi. The deep end borders have two inserted panels of green shawlcloth. It is embroidered in coloured floss silks using satin, stem, long and short, and straight stitches
EG 4474, 240 × 50cm (7ft 9½in × 1ft 8in)

(*left*)

Fragment from a set of hangings, Gujarat (Cambay District), India, made for the English market, 1690s.
White cotton is embroidered with coloured silks using chain stitch. On their sale in the early 1950s, the Ashburnham hangings were divided between the Victoria and Albert Museum, London, the Metropolitan Museum, New York, and the Calico Museum, Ahmedabad, India. It is possible that this fragment entered the Guild's Collection at that period
EG 2505, 62 × 39cm (2ft × 1ft 3¼in) (Photograph: Dudley Moss)

(*right*)

Two shawls, Kashmir, India, c1850.
(*left, with black*) Woven goatswool (*pashmina*) shawl in double interlocking twill tapestry with a few embroidered details
EG 2694, 188 × 200cm (6ft 1¼in × 6ft 7in)
(*right, with red centre*) Woven goatswool (*pashmina*) shawl entirely embroidered with coloured wools using straight and stem stitches
EG 1794, 194 × 205cm (6ft 3½in × 6ft 8in). Given by Mrs Gardner

THE MUGHAL STYLE

The earliest piece in the Collection (EG 613) is a rare fragment from an embroidered hanging of the type made in the Mughal court workshops. The Mughal dynasty, which ruled most of India from the sixteenth to the mid-nineteenth century, was founded by the Central Asian Prince, Babur (1482–1530). He was descended from Genghis Khan and Timur (or Tamburlaine), and it was in recognition of these Mongol origins that Europeans gave the dynasty its title of the Great Mughals (or Mongols). In 1526 Babur defeated the Muslim Afghan rulers of Delhi and made himself Emperor. It is his grandson Akbar (1556–1605) who is generally credited with the successful consolidation of the Mughal empire, which brought cultural cohesion to India's multitude of small Muslim and Hindu kingdoms. Akbar, and his seventeenth-century successors, Jahangir (1605–28), Shah Jahan (1628–58), and Aurangzeb (1658–1707), were rulers whose Islamic court culture was strongly influenced by that of the Safavid dynasty of Persia. Court workshops, based on Persian prototypes, were established at the major imperial cities such as Delhi and Agra. These workshops produced the luxury objects and costly fabrics which made the Mughal court world famous for its conspicuous consumption and display. The marriage of Persian taste with the native Indian traditions of design and craftsmanship, together with the assimilation of some European Renaissance influences, resulted in the new and distinctive decorative style of the Mughal court.

One of the most characteristic elements in this style were semi-naturalistic flower motifs, which were either combined with Persian arabesque ornament or depicted as delicate individual plants. These flowering plant motifs were particularly dominant in textile design throughout the seventeenth and eighteenth centuries, growing ever more complex until they developed into the 'cone-shaped' *buta* familiar to us from nineteenth-century paisley shawl design. In the early period they were frequently used as a row of individual plants along the borders of furnishing textiles, shawls and court girdles, as a diaper of small all-over sprigs on the surface of fabrics used for costume, or in tent hangings and prayer mats as a large flowering plant framed by an arabesque niche.

The introduction of flowering plants as a design motif seems to have been the direct result of Emperor Jahangir's ecstatic reaction to the flora of Kashmir during a visit in the spring of 1620, but is also thought to owe something to the influence of European herbals acquired for the imperial library – the same books which were providing sources of design for contemporary English embroidery. The influence was reciprocal: an early eighteenth-century English bedcover in the Guild's Collection is embroidered with flowering plants, which are so strongly Mughal in style that they must have been directly copied from an imported Indian textile.

EARLY TRADE EMBROIDERIES

The border fragment illustrated (EG 613), which dates from the last quarter of the seventeenth century, is lightly wadded with raw cottonwool, and the ground is quilted in double running stitch. The repeating border of flowering plants is embroidered in fine chain stitch, used in rows as a filling stitch. These two techniques – quilting and chain-stitch embroidery – are characteristic of the earliest Indian embroideries to be imported into Europe. From Bengal in the east, under Portuguese patronage, came quilted white cotton covers worked with pictorial designs in white or (wild) yellow silk using chain stitch. These were produced under Portuguese patronage. The earliest references in European sources to this class of work occur in the early sixteenth century, and examples are preserved in museum collections in India and the West.

Among travellers and traders in the sixteenth century the region of Gujarat, in western India, was more famous than Bengal for its embroidery. Gujarat work seems to have been distinguished from that of Bengal by its use of coloured silks. One of the earliest specimens to survive is a large embroidered bedcover preserved at Hardwick Hall in Derbyshire, where it is recorded among other Indian embroideries in an inventory of 1603.

When the English East India Company began trading in Gujarat in the early seventeenth century, one of its objectives was to acquire embroideries and painted cloths, or chintzes, for resale. There are many references to Indian quilts and hangings in the Company's London sale records from the middle of the century. It was the skilled techniques of embroidery and painting, together with vibrant dye colours unknown in Europe, which found especial favour. But the Indian designs were not always to the English taste, so the custom grew for the

THE INDIAN TRADITION

Company factors to supply English designs to the Indian embroiderers and chintz painters. These designs for bed hangings and wall hangings combined large-scale foliage patterns with motifs reflecting the enthusiasm at the time for chinoiserie. In the hands of Indian craftsmen, the resulting textiles were a unique blend of influences of East and West. In much the same way, the Dutch, French and Portuguese trading companies commissioned designs to meet the demands of their own home markets.

In the Guild's Collection is a fragment (EG 2505) from a set of hangings made in Gujarat for Ashburnham House, Sussex, in the late seventeenth century. The design was taken from an English embroidery pattern which also survives in a crewelwork version. The family also purchased Indian chintz hangings made to the same design. This piece, and the examples of eighteenth-century trade embroidery fabrics also illustrated (EG 2324, 2982) show the quality of technique and delicacy of colour which so impressed Western contemporaries. The chain stitch is exceptionally fine, and the lines of stitches are placed so close as to impart a sheen to the surface of the motifs.

The waistcoat (EG 2982) is an example of chain-stitch work from Bengal using unbleached wild silk on white cotton – a characteristic combination of materials in this region up to the nineteenth century. The all-over pattern, with its rocky hillocks and pagodas, is a typical Chinese-inspired European design. Quilting in chain and back stitch using dyed yellow silk was a popular feature of English embroidery from around 1690 to 1730, and must have been largely inspired by such imported wild-silk embroideries from Bengal. A nineteenth-century example of the use of wild silk with chain-stitch embroidery is shown in the Sari end (EG 3254) from Bengal (modern Bangladesh).

(*right background*)

FRAGMENT OF EMBROIDERED fabric, Gujarat, India, worked as piece goods for the European market, mid-eighteenth century. This is white cotton woven with a small diaper pattern and embroidered with coloured silks using chain stitch. Fabric designs of this kind were also produced as chintz, and were very popular in Europe both for gowns and for bedhangings. Such patterns were not made for the Indian market, where garment pieces were usually decorated with repeating sprig designs
EG 2324, 89 × 86cm (2ft 10¾in × 2ft 9½in). Given by Lady Stokes (Photograph: Dudley Moss)

(*foreground*)

WAISTCOAT, English *c*1760s, the embroidery executed in Bengal, India, *c*1720. This man's waistcoat is made up from piece-good embroidery worked in chain stitch in pale yellow wild silk on white cotton, to a chinoiserie design for the European market. The work is somewhat coarser than the Gujarati chain-stitch embroideries
EG 2982, length 78cm (2ft 6½in). Given by Mrs Skelton

SARI END, Bengal, late nineteenth century. Fine white hand-woven cotton with chequers woven in wild silk, and broad woven borders of wild silk. The embroidered floral ornament is worked in wild silk using chain stitch, and fine white cotton using pulled-thread openwork stitchery
EG 3254, 102 × 159cm (3ft 3¾in × 5ft 2in). Given by Mrs K. Harris (Photograph: Dudley Moss)

SHAWLS

A wool-weaving industry had been established in Kashmir as early as the eleventh century, and was certainly producing much-prized shawls by the reign of Emperor Akbar. He encouraged and improved the industry, and Kashmir shawls became one of the most luxurious court textiles, often given as gifts to the nobility. Men wearing Kashmir shawls as sashes, or folded over the shoulder, are seen again and again in paintings depicting court life up to the eighteenth century. These shawls were made from the fine inner fleece (*pashmina*) of the Himalayan goat, which made them very soft and light, yet warm. They were woven using a complex double-interlocking tapestry technique. Their manufacture, from spinning and dyeing to weaving, was entirely carried out by men and was time consuming and labour intensive, which of course contributed to the value of the shawls and the esteem in which they were held. At the end of the eighteenth century they became essential fashionable wear in the West, and remained so for the best part of a century. As a result Kashmir shawl design began to reflect European taste, and the Mughal designs with their delicate flower-spray borders, were gradually replaced in the first half of the nineteenth century by increasingly complex and opulent European-inspired patterns, dominated by the *buta*, the 'cone' (paisley) motif now regarded as the classic shawl pattern.

The embroidered Kashmir shawl was developed at the beginning of the nineteenth century in response both to the increased export demand and the use of more complex designs. Prior to this, embroidery had been used only to outline woven patterns, or to join various elements of a woven shawl. The embroidered shawls were cheaper than the tapestry-woven versions, being quicker to produce and, at least at the beginning, not subject to local tax. It is said that the wholly embroidered shawl was

S HAWL (detail), India, second half of the nineteenth century. The red shawlcloth is from Kashmir, the embroidery professionally worked in north-west India, probably in Delhi. The two end borders are richly embroidered with laid and couched gilt thread, with details worked in blue, green and black silk threads
EG 205. 306 × 134cm (7ft 11¼in × 4ft 4¼in)

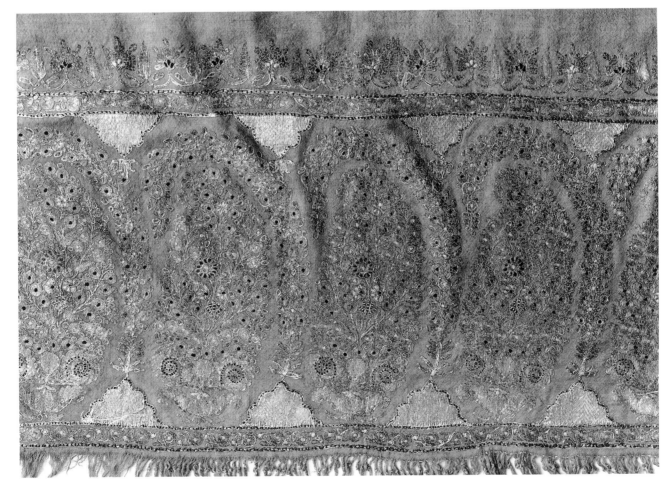

introduced by an Armenian shawl agent, who arranged for Persian embroiderers from Kirman to instruct the Kashmiri workers in the technique of fine wool embroidery upon wool cloth. By the 1830s, thousands of male embroiderers were producing shawls; to the uninformed eye, the best of these are indistinguishable from their tapestry-woven counterparts, as shown on page 119 (EG 2694, 1794).

In the second half of the nineteenth century, the Kashmiri industry faced growing competition, in the export market from European shawl-making centres, and in India from imported factory-made textiles. These factors led them increasingly to adopt coarser and speedier ways of working. From the middle of the century, oppressive local taxation caused thousands of Kashmiri shawl weavers and embroiderers to migrate south to Amritsar, and to other towns of north and western India, where they influenced the style of local textile workers. This gave rise to a variety of types of late-nineteenth- and early-twentieth-century north-Indian shawl work, which was rarely of the fine quality of the original

Kashmiri work, but was clearly descended from it.

One characteristic class of shawl embroidery grew up at Delhi using softly coloured, or entirely cream, floss silks. The designs usually incorporated *buta*s and stylised floral borders, executed in satin, long and short, stem and straight stitches. The example on page 117 (EG 4474) is worked on Kashmiri-made, plain shawl cloth, but later examples are also found on other fabrics, including machine-made net.

Other north-west-Indian embroiderers turned to a loose, bold form of chain stitch for working covers and shawls, drawing, whether consciously or unconsciously, on the earlier chain-stitch tradition of the Gujarat region. Towards the end of the century they produced brightly coloured, but often crudely drawn, *buta*-patterned shawls. Chain stitch and its variants were also used for a class of tablecovers with pictorial subjects as shown on page 127 (EG 3212). The precise origin of the latter is unknown, but they may be descended from the fine chain-stitch embroideries produced by court workshops at Jaipur, Rajasthan, in the eighteenth century.

GOLD AND SILVER EMBROIDERY

As the centralised power of the Mughals slowly diminished during the eighteenth century, many craftsmen left the imperial workshops to seek patronage at provincial courts. The craftsmen further disseminated the Mughal style, which combined with many local urban textile traditions, and can still be detected in elements of village and tribal embroideries in this century.

One of the skills which had been much in demand in the Mughal workshops was embroidery in gold and silver. Although the demand for the richest categories of work diminished, metal-thread embroidery became established as one of the most important forms of professional urban embroidery, which to some extent it remains today. There were traditionally several classes of this work: the heaviest, *karchop*, was laid and couched work over thick cotton padding, and was used for horse and elephant trappings. *Zardosi* was slightly lighter, but

still padded, laid and couched work, on velvet or satin, used also for saddlecloths, and for floorspreads. These techniques are reputed to have been introduced into India by the Portuguese, and in fact the methods differ little from heavy-quality metal-thread embroidery produced in many other parts of the world. *Kalabatan* was the term used to embrace a range of light, gold and silver embroidery using couched metal threads, wires, purls, and spangles, upon silk, cotton, wool or muslin. It was used for costume, covers and items of personal use. The shawl illustrated (EG 205), with its opulent *buta* worked in laid and couched gold thread, falls into this last category, while the cover (EG 202) given to the Guild by Queen Mary is probably more appropriately classed as *zardosi* because of its padded motifs. Both these types of embroidery are still produced in India today, although modern tinsels have replaced gold and silver in the threads.

CHAMBA RUMAL

The *rumal*s of the tiny kingdom of Chamba in the western Himalayas represent a provincial court embroidery tradition. These covers for ceremonial gifts worked by women of the court as a pastime are particularly associated with Chamba, but they were also made at Kangra,

Bilaspur, Mandi, Kulu and other places in the Pahari Hills, during the eighteenth and nineteenth centuries.

It is thought that the designs were often prepared for the women by court artists. In their style and subject matter, Chamba *rumal*s were related to the contemporary

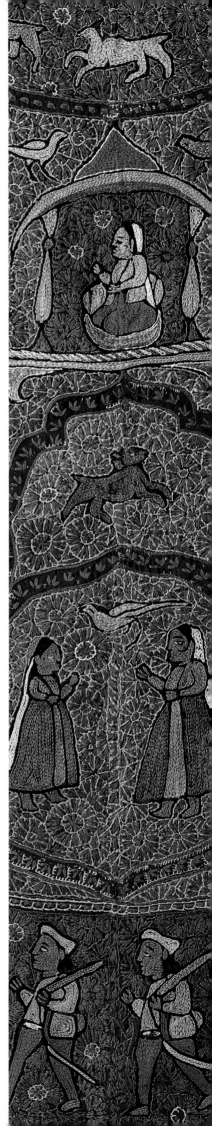

(*above*)

COVER, north India, late nineteenth, early twentieth century.
The field is of pink silk brocaded with gold thread and the borders are of plain pink silk embroidered with a range of laid and couched gilt purls and spangles. The cover is fringed with gilt thread and seed pearls
EG 202, 950 × 225cm
(30ft 10½in × 7ft 3¾in).
Given by Queen Mary (Photograph: Embroiderers' Guild)

(*right*)

TABLECOVER (detail), northern or north-western India, c1880s.
Cotton is embroidered with coloured floss silks using chain, open chain, and stem stitches. It is professional work. The cover is square with two concentric medallions and the borders and compartments contain a variety of animals, and figures engaged in courtly pastimes. An army marches around the edge of the larger medallion and the corners contain winged *deva* (Hindu gods)
EG 3212, 179cm (5ft 10in) square

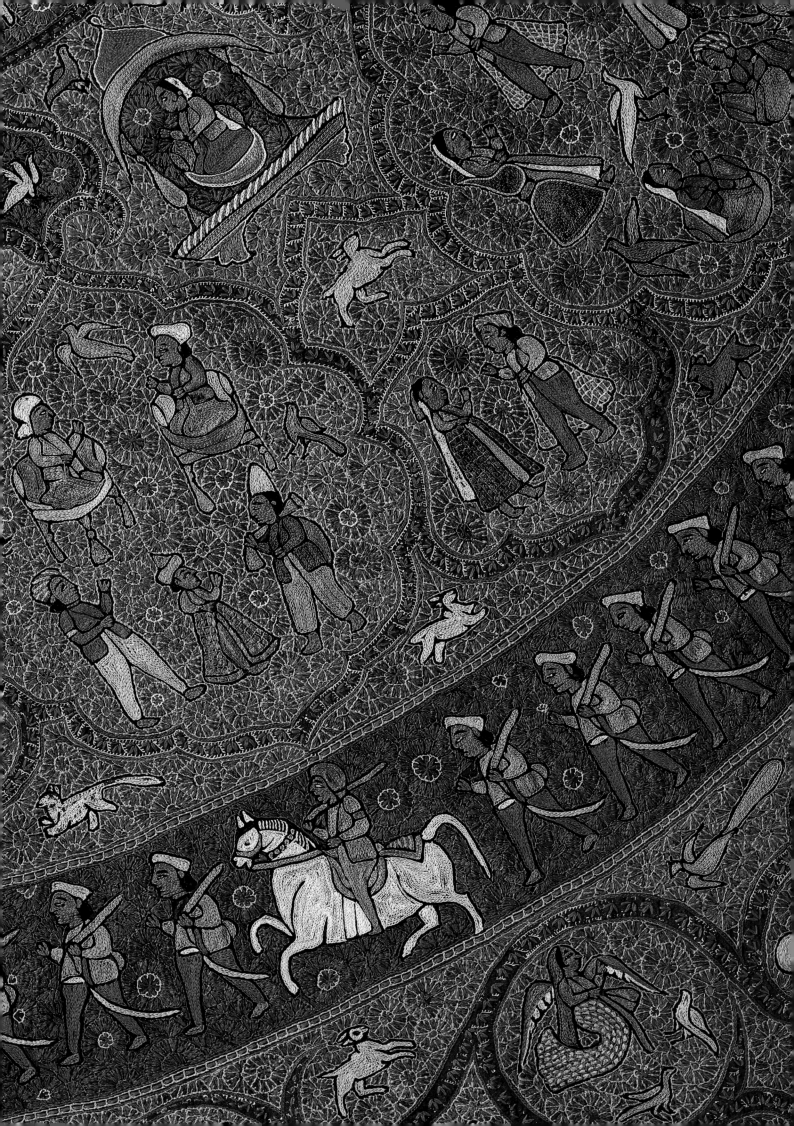

THE INDIAN TRADITION

local Pahari school of miniature painting and later, even more closely, to the murals of the Rang Mahal, or 'painted palace', at Chamba, which was built to house the women's quarters in the first half of the nineteenth century. The themes illustrated on the *rumal*s echo those of the paintings: stories of Krishna and his love for Radha, social scenes such as marriage processions, and hunting scenes. The design of the Rang Mahal murals is echoed in the division of these scenes into compartments, and in the floral arabesque borders which divide them.

The embroidery technique used is a long double-darning stitch worked in soft floss silks. The motifs were usually outlined in black silk and the details highlighted in flat silver wire (*badla*).

*R*UMAL (cover for a ceremonial gift), Chamba, India, nineteenth century. Hand-spun and hand-woven cotton is embroidered with coloured floss silks using double darning stitch and stem stitch. Some details are worked in flat silver wire (*badla*). Much of the black silk used to work the border outlines and scrolling flower stems has rotted, revealing the original drawing lines. These *rumal* were made as a pastime by women in the court harem and were given as gifts or used to cover gifts. The scenes depict the god Krishna playing at hide and seek and archery with his companions, and awaiting the arrival of his lover Radha who approaches his pavilion with a garland. Modern, commercially made Chamba *rumals* can be distinguished by their machine-woven cloth, cruder drawing, and brighter dyes
*EG 3263. 76.5 cm (2ft 6in) square
(Photograph: Embroiderers' Guild)*

Chamba *rumal*s have been revived in this century as a local commercial handicraft, and there are two examples (not illustrated) of these later pieces in the Guild's Collection. They can usually be distinguished from older examples by their machine-woven cloth, cruder drawing, and brighter, synthetic dyes.

CHIKAN WORK

Another class of embroidery which developed to some extent in response to local court patronage was *chikan* work. Sheila Paine, in the first thorough study of this whitework embroidery, has shown how *chikan*, with its precise repertoire of stitches, differs from the wide range of nineteenth-century Indo-European whitework produced both for export and for the resident British

Two uncut cap crowns (from a group of five), probably Lucknow, India, late nineteenth or early twentieth century.
Chikan work: white cotton muslin embroidered with untwisted white cotton thread using chain, running, double back, and stem stitches. (For a detailed description of the stitches used in *chikan* embroidery, some of which have no European equivalents, see *Chikan Embroidery* by Sheila Paine)
Group: EG 4933, diameters of caps illustrated 14.5 and 13.5cm (5½ and 5¼in)

(*above*)

WOMAN'S ROBE, (*pushk kurta*), Baluchistan, modern Pakistan, late nineteenth or early twentieth century.
Made for a Brahui woman, probably by a professional embroiderer in Quetta, it is of green silk with inset panels of cotton, thickly embroidered with laid and couched gilt threads and mirror glass. Details are picked out in coloured silks. Gilt braid is applied
EG 3266, length 116cm (3ft 9¼in). Given by Mrs Hewitt-Pitt

(*left*)

HEADCLOTH (detail), Hazara district, Punjab, India, early twentieth century.
Of hand-woven brick-red cotton embroidered with orange, cream and green floss silks using darning stitch on counted threads, this work is generally described as *phulkari*, although this particular class is more correctly termed *bagh*, and is a cloth prepared especially for ceremonial occasions such as marriages
EG 23 1982, 260 × 140cm (8ft 5½in × 4ft 6½in). Purchased

(*above*)

WOMAN'S BODICE PANEL, Sind, modern Pakistan, early twentieth century.
Red and green pieced cotton is embroidered with coloured silks using open chain, interlacing, straight and buttonhole stitches, with applied mirror glass
EG 2701, length 60cm (1ft 11½in). Given by Mrs Keeton

community. *Chikan* seems to have had its roots in a white-embroidered muslin industry which developed at the end of the eighteenth century as a less-expensive imitation of the famous pattern-woven white muslins of Dacca (*jamdani*). It was stimulated by the European fashion for sprigged muslin.

This early whitework was principally cotton, embroidered in the length with small repeating motifs executed in a simple running stitch (*tepchi*). By the second half of the nineteenth century, it seems to have developed into the form we know as *chikan* work: complex and delicate designs based on *butas*, stylised floral motifs and tendrils, executed in a variety of stitches, and featuring pulledwork known as *jali*. In Bengal, the heart of the Indian muslin industry, *chikan* embroidery was produced principally as piece goods for trade, while in Lucknow, under the patronage of the Nawabs of Oudh, it was used to decorate high-quality costume pieces. It has now entirely disappeared from Bengal, but is still an important occupation in modern Lucknow.

PHULKARI EMBROIDERY

The rural embroideries of Baluchistan and north-western Punjab, now both in modern Pakistan, are predominantly geometric in style, and based upon counted-thread techniques, reflecting the stronger influence of the Islamic non-figurative tradition. The *phulkari* (literally, 'flowering work') embroidery of the Punjab was traditionally produced by women of the Jat peoples, both Hindu and Muslim, to decorate headcloths, hangings and covers. In the eastern Punjab, many *phulkari* include stylised figurative motifs such as animals, flowers, and scenes from daily life, but those of the west are always geometric. The rich, all-over patterns of the type illustrated (EG 23 1982) are more properly termed *bagh* (literally, 'garden') and were special cloths produced for ceremonial occasions. After the birth of a child, the paternal grandmother would initiate preparations for working a *bagh* to be used at the marriage of the child when it grew up. It might take ten years to complete, despite some work being carried out every day. *Bagh* of the finest quality and complexity came from the Hazara region in the extreme north-west Punjab.

All *phulkari* and *bagh* were worked on hand-woven cotton, often dyed rust red or indigo blue. Three or four of the narrow loom widths were joined lengthwise to make a cover or headcloth. The most striking characteristic of the work is that the counted-thread darning stitch was always worked from the back. Hardly any silk shows on the reverse of these embroideries, but on the face the closely blocked floss silk transforms the homespun cotton into a luxurious, light reflecting fabric. As with other kinds of work, *phulkari* has died out as a home craft. It has been revived for commercial purposes but the modern embroideries are inferior both in materials and workmanship to the older examples.

ROBES
FROM BALUCHISTAN

The same counted-thread embroidery, which relies upon textural effect rather than varied colour and motif, is seen on the magnificent woman's robe, or *pushk kurta*, from Baluchistan (EG 3272). It is an example of the garments made by women of the Brahui peoples who live in the remote Brahui Hills to the extreme north of Baluchistan. These loose robes (worn with trousers) have a characteristic long pocket with a pointed top at the centre front, which, like the bodice panel and sleeves, is usually richly embroidered. The Guild is fortunate to possess six examples of women's robes, all dating from the late nineteenth or early twentieth century. The example decorated with gold embroidery (EG 3266) was the work of a professional embroiderer, probably at Quetta, the major town of Baluchistan, not far from the Afghan border.

WOMAN'S ROBE (*pushk kurta*), Baluchistan, modern Pakistan, late nineteenth or early twentieth century.
Made by and for a woman of the Brahui tribe, this is of cream silk with inset panels of white cotton embroidered with dark red silk using satin stitch and closed herringbone stitch on counted threads. The Guild owns a second almost identical garment
EG 3272. length 114cm (3ft 8½in)
Given by Mrs Hewitt-Pitt
(Photograph: Embroiderers' Guild)

FRAGMENT OF A SKIRT piece, Kutch, Gujarat State, India, early twentieth century. Red silk satin is embroidered with red, black, yellow and white silks using interlacing stitch and some chain stitch, with applied mirror glass. Interlacing stitch is found in rural embroideries to a greater or lesser extent across the whole western region, from Sind down to Kathiawar
EG 2648, 26 × 48cm (10in × 1ft 6¾in). Given by Miss K. Paget

Woman's tunic (*kanjro*) (back shown), Thano Bula Khan, Sind, modern Pakistan, early twentieth century. This tunic is made of pieced silk and cotton fabrics. Most of the front and back surfaces are thickly embroidered with coloured silk and cotton threads, applied mirror glass, spangles and braid. These richly decorated garments were made for weddings, although subsequently worn as everyday dress. Two pockets on the neck opening are stuffed with herbs intended to bring good fortune *EG 24 1982, length 83cm (2ft 8½in). Purchased*

WOMAN'S ROBE (*pushk kurta*), Baluchistan, late nineteenth century, early twentieth century.
This was made by Mochi embroiderers in Kutch for a woman of the Brahui tribe. Deep purple silk taffeta is embroidered with brightly coloured silks using chain stitch made with an *ari* or hook. This robe has twice been shortened
EG 3273, length 120cm (3ft 10¾in). Given by Mrs Hewitt-Pitt (Photograph: Embroiderers' Guild)

URBAN EMBROIDERY
IN GUJARAT

Another of these robes (EG 3273) must have been pro- duced much further south in Kutch, Gujarat state, since it is an example of professional embroidery made by mem- bers of the Mochi caste. The Mochis were traditionally cobblers and leatherworkers, and it is not known when they began to practise embroidery on silk. Certainly embroidery on leather was long established in the region, observed by Marco Polo among the products of western India at the end of the thirteenth century. The distinguishing feature of Mochi embroidery was that it was chain stitch, worked with an *ari*, a hooked tool like a cross between a cobbler's awl and a tambour hook. The technique used was identical to that of European tambourwork, except that the *ari*, and the stitches it pro- duces, are much finer. In the long and diverse tradition of Indian chain-stitch embroideries, only this class of work is produced with a hook and not a needle. The distinc- tion is easily established by examining the reverse of the embroidery.

Another class of professional urban embroidery

unique to Gujarat was the *chinai* embroidery, an example of which is illustrated (EG 4368), produced by the small community of immigrant Chinese embroiderers at Surat in the nineteenth and early twentieth centuries. They worked almost exclusively for the Parsees – Persian communities which had settled in the region centuries before – embroidering for them garments and costume- trimming borders sold by the length. Although these embroideries use a selection of classic Chinese stitches, including the so-called 'Peking knot', together with motifs derived from Chinese design, they are not quite the same as anything produced in China.

CHILD'S TUNIC (detail), Surat, Gujarat, India, late nineteenth, early twentieth century.
This was made for the Parsee community by Chinese immigrant embroiderers. Red Chinese silk with striped weave is embroidered with white twisted silk using satin, stem and straight stitches
EG 4368. length 69cm (2ft 3in).
Given by Mrs Hewitt-Pitt
(Photograph: Embroiderers' Guild)

THREE PURSES, Banjara or Lambadi tribes, Deccan Plateau, India, twentieth century.
These are of cotton, embroidered with coloured cotton threads using counted thread stitches. One purse is decorated with bunches of cowrie shells, and another with large disks of mirror glass tassels
EG 283, 284 and 285 1983, largest 12 × 20cm (4¾ × 8in). Purchased

FLOORMAT, Jessore, East Bengal, modern Bangladesh, late nineteenth or early twentieth century.
Layered cotton cloth is quilted through all thicknesses with coloured cottons using running stitch
EG 5 1985. 113 × 83cm (3ft 8in × 2ft 8¼in). Purchased

RURAL EMBROIDERIES OF WESTERN INDIA

The embroideries made by the numerous and diverse rural communities of western India – the southern Punjab, Sind and modern Gujarat state (which includes Kutch, Saurashtra and Kathiawar) – still represent a source of some of the richest folk embroidery in the world. For centuries this region saw a steady migration and interchange of a wide variety of groups, both Muslim and Hindu, whether nomads or settled agriculturalists. The Pakistan/India border now separates Sind from Gujarat, but this has not created a sharp division in the ethnic and cultural traits which link the whole region. In all these communities, embroidered textiles have traditionally played a central role in costume and in domestic decoration, in ritual and ceremony. They reflect family status and wealth in a society with a subsistence economy and limited personal possessions.

Across the whole region, many patterns and techniques are held in common (such as the use of mirror glass or *shisha* work); nevertheless, in detail, designs vary endlessly from group to group and family to family. The same applies to the form of embroidered garments, which broadly follows the pattern of bodices, skirts and head cloths for women, and shoulder cloths, turban cloths and ceremonial sashes for men. The shape and decoration of these, however, is particular to each social group, and may also reflect the status of the wearer within that group. Embroidery is used too to decorate a wide range of domestic and ceremonial textiles, such as wall hangings and friezes, bedding covers, wrappers, and door hangings.

Unlike most urban embroidery produced in India, these rural embroideries are entirely a homecraft executed by women for the use of their own families. Geometric patterns and abstract motifs tend to dominate in

the north of the region, in Sind, but are increasingly mixed with figurative motifs – human and divine figures, elephants, peacocks, parrots and flowers – the further south the embroideries are produced, and work from Kathiawar is particularly rich in pictorial motifs.

Two embroidered garments from Sind – a woman's bodice panel (EG 2701) on page 131 and a woman's tunic (EG 24 1982), page 135 – exemplify the special brilliance and complexity of embroideries produced in this area. Both are decorated with disks of mirror glass, which are applied using a form of herringbone stitch worked around a loop. In the case of the tunic, the embroidery is further enlivened by a variety of applied braids and spangles. Many of the stitches used would be familiar to Western embroiderers, although they are often used in unfamiliar ways. A method of outlining motifs, which is seen on both pieces, uses what looks like a row of upright straight stitches, each one of which is crossed with a short straight stitch placed at right angles. This is *vell* stitch, produced in one sequence – another of the techniques found very widely across western India.

The borders of the bodice panel are worked with squares of interlacing stitch, made by interweaving the thread around a previously worked base grid of stitches. The same stitch is used almost exclusively to work the design on the fragment of a skirt piece from Kutch (EG 2648), page 134. Curiously, the other principal manifestation of this stitch is on late medieval German embroideries but there is no known connection between the two. Unlike the robust decoration of the Sind garments, the design of this skirt piece still reflects something of the sophisticated Mughal design tradition; the repeating motifs of the field, although highly stylised, are descended from the Mughal flowering plant.

APPLIQUÉ, PATCHWORK AND QUILTING

Appliqué and patchwork are common techniques throughout western India, as well as in southern India. As in other societies, they stem from the need for thrifty reuse of fabric from old garments and covers. The area best known for this class of work is that represented by modern Gujarat state, where it is used for cushions,

mattresses, hangings, and other household decorations, as well as umbrellas, bullock covers and cart covers. There is a small cover (*chakla*) in the Collection (EG 41 1983), not illustrated, which is an example of appliqué or *katab* work. It was made by stitching cut-out shapes of coloured cotton to a white cotton ground, turning the raw edges under and attaching these with running stitch. Traditionally, *chakla* (which may also be decorated using other techniques) were used by a bride to wrap round the articles of her dowry and were later hung upon the walls of her new home.

The decorative quilting of Bengal known as *kantha*, an example of which is illustrated (EG 5 1985), also depended upon re-use of old fabrics. It is believed that this work developed during the nineteenth century among Hindu women of the poor *dhobi* caste (washerwomen), who were able to obtain saris too fragile to withstand further washing. The *kantha* were made by layering several old white saris, and quilting them together using threads drawn from the coloured borders of the same saris. For this reason the colour range of the old examples is very limited – mainly blue and red. The quilting is executed in fine running stitch, worked in parallel straight or curved lines, and covering the whole surface. The designs were created by the women themselves and feature popular motifs of Hindu myth and ritual, scenes from everyday life, animals and plants, which are usually grouped around a central lotus medallion. They are related to the tradition of the complex ritual drawings which the Hindu women of the region still draw on the floors and mud walls of their homes in rice paste. Like other forms of folk embroidery, *kantha* work has been revived in this century, under the Bengal Home Industries Association. The modern pieces are worked on new fabrics using a wider range of coloured threads than was used over a century ago.

GYPSY WORK

We cannot conclude this selection without mentioning a group of bags (EG 283, 284, 285 1983) made by the women of the Banjara and Lambadi tribes, nomadic gypsies of north-western Indian origin who are now found all over western and southern India. They work as casual labourers, second-hand dealers and itinerant dancers and musicians. The women decorate their own costume, and articles for sale, with embroidery and by the ingenious use of patched materials, applied cowrie shells, buttons, metal ornaments, tassels, and mirror disks (the latter often used in much larger pieces than in western Indian embroidery).

The range of stitches found in Banjara and Lambadi work is very wide, but one of the most characteristic techniques is fine, counted-thread, all-over embroidery (always executed from the back of the fabric), which is the nearest parallel found in Indian embroidery to European canvaswork.

CHAPTER 5

EUROPEAN PEASANT EMBROIDERY

Heirlooms from the Eighteenth and Nineteenth Centuries

Jennifer Wearden

IN MAINLAND EUROPE until recently the term 'peasant' indicated families who either owned or were tenants of a smallholding where they raised crops and animals. Peasant communities were normally self sufficient in all their basic needs but their continued existence was precariously dependent on not only the vagaries of the harvest but also on the stability of the families which formed the village.

The community survived on the interdependence and continuation of the families and needed to nourish a strong sense of its own separate identity in order to discourage migration. For this reason peasant communities evolved complex customs and etiquette to control the important events of life – birth, marriage, death, inheritance and so on – and it is in the context of such special occasions ('special' for the community as well as for the individuals) that highly decorated clothes and furnishings were used.

As with all ceremonial items, even functional ones, the cut and ornamentation became formalised and traditional. The garments or furnishings were not stylish ones to be discarded as and when fashion dictated, but were often expensive pieces made or purchased by naturally provident peasants, intended to last at least one lifetime and usually passed down to the next generation as treasured heirlooms. This is not to say that major artistic movements such as the Baroque, the Rococo and the Classical revival of the early nineteenth century had no effect on peasant art – certain motifs can be seen which owe their origin to these international influences – but they are often far removed in time. Poor, or non-existent, communication networks, a lack of journals and fashion plates and no universal education meant that peasant communities received new ideas from the cities long after they had first been introduced there.

MAN'S SLEEVELESS JACKET, Transylvania, late nineteenth century. Cream suede with red leather appliqué is edged with black wool, decorated with interlaced strips of coloured leather and applied woollen braids, and embroidered with coloured wools, mainly in satin stitch. Traditionally there were marked differences between jackets and waistcoats for men and for women: those for men were white and were trimmed with the straight wool from the legs of the sheep, those for women were dyed a darker colour and were trimmed with curly wool

EG 286 1983, approx 51 × 54cm (1ft 8in × 1ft 9in). Given by the members of Stow-on-the-Wold and Countryside Branch

It is impossible to understand all the complex details of European peasant embroidery. Several thousand pieces have survived, dating from about 1750 (at the earliest) to the 1930s. They were made in an area of the world which covers six and a half million square kilometres (over four million square miles) and which had, at the beginning of the twentieth century, a population of approximately four hundred million people. The scope for variation is enormous and what has survived can never be fully representative. It is not possible to describe or illustrate every sort of design and technique, or to describe the function of every piece and the circumstances under which it would have been made or the traditions surrounding its use. However, by outlining some of the shared features of peasant embroidery and highlighting some specific points, it is possible to hint at the fascination of this type of work and at the complexity and richness of a tradition which is often underrated or ignored. Although most of the embroideries would have been worked within the home by women and girls, large villages often had access to a professional seamstress or tailor who would not only construct complicated outer garments but might also decorate them. In Scandinavia for instance the embroidery on costume was often done by the (male) tailor and in Hungary embroideries on sheepskin were always done by professional craftsmen. These usually lived and worked in small towns to which village people would come to order or purchase a garment.

TECHNIQUES

It is seldom that any unusual technique is encountered in European peasant embroidery. There are counted-thread embroideries which were generally done by copying an existing piece, or from memory or imagination; freehand embroidery for which designs were first drawn out on to the fabric, with very complex ones often being copied from drafted patterns; borders of drawn-thread work which are found on both costume and furnishings; and appliqué, cutwork and the use of braids and cords. Sometimes one or two experienced people in the village would draw the designs for other women. In Protestant parishes in Western Europe the pastor's wife could often provide pattern books and samplers for village women to copy. In Blekinge in eastern Sweden there were skilled embroideresses who travelled from farm to farm designing and embroidering wallhangings for the households. Often several women would co-operate on a large piece or would simply gather together for company, with most embroidery being worked in the winter and early spring when there was less work in the fields. Some Bulgarian villages would hold an exhibition in spring to show the winter's embroidery.

MATERIALS

Unless the community was situated on or near a major trade route and the inhabitants could afford to acquire imported cloth, most fabrics used were woven from locally produced linen and wool; finer materials such as cotton were available from the middle of the nineteenth century onwards and cotton then gradually replaced linen. Anything extra such as lace, ribbons, and in the late nineteenth century gold and silver threads, spangles and glass beads, would have been obtained by barter or would have been bought from pedlars or from fairs. Several unusual but locally available ornaments were worked into embroidery – shells were very popular in Macedonia and, because of the large number of fish ponds in southern Bohemia, people there used layers of fish scales as decoration. Most embroidery was worked with wool which, depending on the breed of sheep and the part of the fleece it came from, could be very glossy and silk like. White linen was generally used whenever white thread was needed. Natural dyestuffs from barks and moss, heathers and other plants were used until they were replaced in the late nineteenth century by synthetic dyes which were imported and sold in many shops. Initially, chemically produced dyestuffs were bought to supplement and enrich traditional colours but as they became cheaper they were used with less discrimination.

FOUR PANELS, Slovakia(?), mid-nineteenth century.
All are cotton embroidered with silk, in satin, running and chain stitches. From the top the colours are: black; red, yellow and black; black, red and pink; red and black. The last three also include chain stitch. Sometimes these panels are still attached to pieces of very tightly pleated fabric and they may have been used to decorate the shoulder or cuff of a garment or may have formed a decorative panel in a cap or headdress. Such borders were removed from old garments to be re-used and were often chopped off larger pieces by collectors
EG 1118, 5 × 14cm (2 × 5½in); EG 4501(10/10), 5.5 × 12.5cm (2¼ × 5in); EG 4501 (7/10), 5 × 13.5cm (2 × 5¼in); EG 4501(9/10), 5 × 14.5cm (2 × 5¾in)

(*above*)

CUSHION COVER, Sweden (Skane), a 1947 copy of a cover dated 1820 with the embroidered initials KOD. Black wool is embroidered with red, green, mauve, pale blue and white wool, and cream and yellow silk, in coarsely worked satin, chain, cross, stem and long and short stitches, and French knots. It is quite common for the ground fabric in such cushions to be taken from an old skirt. Carriage cushions are similar in design and technique but are oblong in shape and usually contain two square designs side by side
EG 2652, 47 × 46cm (1ft 6¼in × 1ft 6in). Given by the NDS

(*right*)

TWO TOWEL BORDERS, Russian, late nineteenth century.
Of bleached linen embroidered with red cotton and blue silk in cross stitch with narrow bands of drawn threadwork, both are embroidered with designs of chickens and with proverbial inscriptions. The border on the left (EG 4487) reads 'Expensive and pretty, Cheap and nasty' and the one on the right (EG 4488) reads 'Complete what you set out to do'; this border is further decorated with an applied band of red cotton
Left: EG 4487, 43 × 39cm (1ft 4¾in × 1ft 3¼in). Right: EG 4488. 40 × 38cm (1ft 3¾in × 1ft 3in)

146

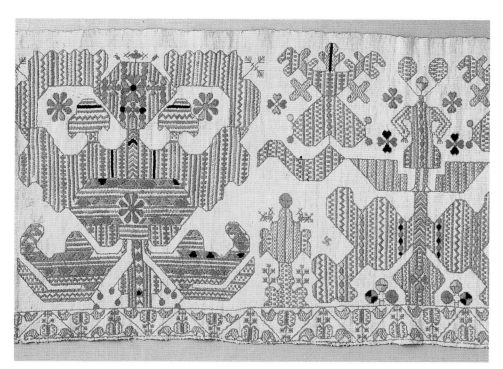

(*left*)

D ETAIL FROM the border of a bedcurtain, Russian (Olonetz Province), late nineteenth century. Unbleached linen is embroidered with red cotton, and black, orange, green, red, blue, brown and yellow wool, in a variety of counted thread stitches and stem and satin stitch. The detail shows a very stylised double-headed eagle (the emblem of the ruling Romanov dynasty), to the left of three female figures which are often said to represent the mother goddess

EG 4492, 35 × 107cm (1ft 1½in × 3ft 5¾in). Given by Mrs Eumosfoporus

DESIGNS

It is probably true to say that the basic designs used were not developed by the peasants themselves but were derived from the major artistic movements – the Renaissance and Baroque and Rococo styles – which first affected European society at its highest level and then percolated gradually through to the lowest. Sometimes, but not often, the direct source of the designs can be located, as with some complicated geometric designs worked in cross stitch which can be traced back to pattern books printed in the sixteenth and seventeenth centuries. Most other designs are anonymously international: flowers of all types were popular, as was the so-called 'tree of life' motif and a design which depicted flowers springing from a vase, flanked by a pair of birds. Christian symbols – such as the pelican feeding its young with its blood, the Agnus Dei and figures from the Old Testament, especially Adam and Eve – are usually found only on furnishings. The variety of geometric designs used as borders for garments is almost endless with each community combining simple motifs in different ways. Sometimes narrow bands or small panels would be worked directly on to the garment, and sometimes they would be worked on loose material and then applied; if a garment was worn out but the embroidered borders were still fresh, these would be cut off and used again. The illustration on page 145 shows examples of panels.

SYMBOLISM AND SIGNIFICANCE

Some people are tempted to search for the symbolism behind patterns in the belief that each motif has a hidden meaning, but it would be misleading to pretend that everything has a mystic dimension. Some do, for instance the 'sharp' motifs found on bedlinen (see below), and sometimes, in Czechoslovakia for instance, embroideries portray local sayings. It is quite entertaining to assign meanings to motifs but it is a deceptively facile game and in the vast majority of cases there is either no meaning or one so shrouded in local mythology, history or literature that outsiders would be at a loss to unravel it. For example, the Hapsburg double-headed eagle appears in many Central European embroideries but does not symbolise an acceptance of Austrian authority; it is said to remind people of the relatively enlightened Emperor Joseph II (1780–90) who abolished serfdom and allowed Protestants slightly more religious freedom. Symbolism, when it does exist, is seldom obvious.

Not only patterns might have a significance beyond their decorative qualities: colour and the disposition of colour on costume could indicate to the informed observer the social standing of the wearer. In the Hungarian town of Kalotaszeg married women wore blouses embroidered with black and unmarried women wore blouses embroidered with red. The embroidered border on an apron could indicate the age group of the wearer in the same area: it was red for girls and young women, yellow for older women and green or black for those women who were said to be 'quite old'. The black caps worn by women in Sárkőz (a district in southern Hungary, by the Danube) were edged with fine white embroidery and the older the woman grew, the narrower the band of embroidery had to become. Colour could also indicate the religious belief of the wearer, with sober shades being worn by Protestants in preference to the Catholics' bright red and yellow; in Kecskemét in Hungary the furriers always put more red on the *suba* (cloak) of Catholics and more black and blue on those of Calvinists. However, these subtleties were usually only of very local significance.

TROUSSEAUS AND DOWRIES

Much thought and skill was lavished on the adornment of the home and especially on the bed. The style and quantity of furniture and furnishings varied from one area to another but, generally speaking, the main room (sometimes called the clean room) claimed most attention – the bed was placed in this room, which therefore formed both a living and sleeping room. Beautiful embroidered bedlinen was a feature of most houses and it made up the larger part of a bride's trousseau.

On the day before the wedding her trousseau and dowry were carried openly through the village to the bridegroom's house, and her status and that of her family were dependent on the skill with which the pieces had been assembled. Embroidered clothes were included –

blouses, chemises, aprons, headkerchiefs and shawls – as were towels, tablecloths (in Eastern Europe these were not as common as bedlinen and were sometimes used by women as shawls and even as shrouds), sheets, bedcovers, pillowcases, cushion covers and wall hangings. Other articles which had their specific use, sometimes only for certain occasions (marriage, birth, churching, christening or funeral) such as bed curtains, babies' christening clothes, a churching shawl and altar cloths (most houses included a corner shelf which acted as a shrine) might also be included. In the Tyrol the trousseau included embroidered shutter-cloths which were laid on the window shutters when a death occurred. In Eastern Europe special covers would be included to be used at Easter, when cakes and decorated eggs would be offered to family and guests. Embroidered gloves were a necessary addition in Northern Europe. In some areas of Norway the trousseau had to include certain embroidered presents for the new mother-in-law and Russian brides had to give embroidered handkerchiefs or towels as presents to relatives and guests according to their social position and degree of affinity. In many areas of Europe the bride-to-be had to embroider a shirt for her future husband; it would be worn on their wedding day and often never again until it was used as his shroud. It may have taken mother, daughter and female relatives years to prepare the trousseau, but unless the family were poor there would be enough of everything to last the girl's lifetime.

BEDLINEN

In many areas the wealth of a bride was counted in the number of embroidered pillows in her dowry. These, although piled high on the bed, and often the aim was to make them reach the ceiling, were never used (unless it was to support the recently dead during a period of mourning); under other circumstances they concealed plainer pillows which were used every day. Sheets were made from two widths of fabric joined lengthwise, sometimes with a decorative insertion. Although the style of decoration on sheets varied from region to region, the disposition of the embroidered borders was fairly consistent throughout Europe, with a broad band along one narrow end and either nothing or occasionally a thin band along the other. The decoration of pillows and cushions is more varied as they were used in different ways in different regions: if they were to be stacked on top of one another (on a bed, for example) the tendency was to decorate one end only, with an embroidered

CUSHION COVER, west Hungary, a twentieth-century copy of an eighteenth- or nineteenth-century cover.
This is of linen, embroidered with blue cotton mainly in satin and stem stitch. The design would have been drawn on the linen with ink made from lampblack or soot and it shows a combination of European and Ottoman influences, with the carnations and pomegranates coming from the East and the central spray and paired birds coming from the West *EG 3843. 47 × 81cm (1ft 6¼in × 2ft 7½in). Given by the NDS*

DETAIL OF a triangular border for a fichu, Austrian, late eighteenth century.
Fine silk net is worked with coloured silks in a variety of counted thread stitches, giving a totally reversible embroidery. Although the beautifully drawn pattern includes many European motifs such as the wheatsheaf, ribbons tied into bows, a male and female figure harvesting, both the technique and the layout of the narrow and wide borders are typically Ottoman and indicate the widespread nature of Ottoman influences in Europe. This embroidery would have been worked professionally, either to order or for sale in a shop or market
EG 2 1990, each side 16 × 77cm (6¼in × 2ft 6in)

APRON, Hungarian (Mezökövesd region), late nineteenth century.
Heavy black satin ground is joined to a panel of black velvet and embroidered with shades of red, pink and blue, and orange, yellow and grey, mainly in satin stitch, trimmed with machine-made fringes. Throughout the nineteenth century the Matyó people of this area were noted for their colourful embroidery and for their striking costumes despite the fact it was an overpopulated and impoverished region where both men and women were forced to find work as seasonal farmhands on distant estates. Such narrow aprons were worn by young girls and by young men. Tradition says that the aprons of girls are decorated with nine roses and those of men with seven roses; however such rules do not seem to apply to this example which has five
EG 3897, 96 × 90cm (3ft 1½in × 2ft 11½in) (Photograph: Embroiderers' Guild)

151

border, but if the whole of the cushion or pillow were to show, one side would be entirely covered with an embroidered design or pattern. Two cushion covers are illustrated, one from Hungary (EG 3843), page 149 and one from Sweden (EG 2652), page 146. Swedish carriage cushions were so called because they were placed on seats when the family drove to church. There is a story of a farmer's daughter in Scania who had *sixty* carriage cushions in her dowry in the 1830s. Not every family could afford such extravagance but it is a measure of the importance attached to the textile part of a girl's dowry.

As the bed was in the main room it was curtained off with special hangings during a confinement and for six weeks after the birth of a child. These bedcurtains were meant to provide privacy (in Moravia a panel of openwork was humanely included so that the mother could see into the room). They were also to ward off evil so the embroidered designs often include 'sharp' motifs – an axe, a fork, a row of pointed teeth – in order to stab vampires and harpies who might otherwise harm the mother and child. A detail of a Russian bedcurtain (EG 4492) is illustrated on page 147.

Sometimes the scenes are narrative rather than symbolic and depict events connected with the arrival of a child, the bringing of food, the coming of friends, the churching. In parts of what is now Czechoslovakia some bedcurtains are embroidered with motifs of stags and deer which refer to two local sayings: 'May your little boy have a fine build and carry himself like a stag' and 'May your little daughter grow like an apple tree and soon run like a deer'. The Russian towel borders on page 147 are also embroidered with proverbial inscriptions.

COSTUME

On examination there is less embroidery on peasant costume than first impressions might convey – visual impact was created by the skilled use of applied braids and silk ribbons, by frills and edgings of lace, and by the use of colourful woven and printed fabrics. The parts of the costume which were embroidered varied considerably from region to region, but generally speaking, embroidery was found only where it would show to greatest effect – on the shoulders and sleeves, around the neck, on the chest, round the hem of the garment, on the collar and cuffs and sometimes along the seams. Effort would not be wasted on areas which were to be covered by another garment.

Everyday dress, especially in summer, would consist simply of a shift (or blouse and skirt) and an apron for women, and a shirt and trousers for men, with sleeveless waistcoats worn for warmth. These garments had to be durable and were normally made from sturdy material and if they were decorated it was usually in a subdued manner, with colour and exuberance being reserved for the Sunday or festival costumes such as the Hungarian apron on page 151 (EG 3897).

In Northern Europe, where communities tended to be more affluent than they were in the east, detailed and complicated rules developed to govern the type of dress to be worn on different Sundays of the year: the finest garments would be worn on the most important feasts, but the seasons of Lent and Advent required a sober outfit and full mourning was to be worn on Good Friday.

As a general rule it seems that the more affluent a community was, the less ostentatious was its embroidery. In Western and Northern Europe it was concentrated on simple accessories like gloves or aprons, while in the east, where the majority of people could afford no more than one special outfit, embroidery appeared more frequently on main garments – dresses, skirts, blouses and shirts – as well as on accessories.

CAPS

Throughout most of European society in the nineteenth century it was customary for married women to cover their heads with a cap, scarf or more elaborate head-dress, and in peasant communities the 'capping' of the bride was almost the climax of wedding ceremonies, being a clear sign of the woman's changed status. In some regions a special cap or head-dress would be made for the ceremony: in parts of what is now Czechoslovakia it was the duty of the mother to make her daughter's bridal cap, which was carefully laid aside after the wedding until the day of her death, when it was again placed on her head. While a simple cap or scarf would be used for everyday wear, special head-dresses for Sundays and feastdays were often elaborately embroidered cloths sometimes pinned on to complex constructions of every

HEADSCARF, south-west Hungary, mid-nineteenth century.
Cotton ground, with a central insertion of starched and pleated bobbin lace and two side panels of blue silk stitched on to card, is embroidered with white cotton and black silk in satin, padded satin, stem, chain, running, cross, buttonhole and couched stitches. Two initials (MR?) are embroidered on the pointed end; the heart motif used in this embroidery was very popular in all forms of peasant art
EG 120 1987, 69 × 190cm (2ft 3in × 6ft 2in). Given by Miss Clough

imaginable shape made of parchment, wire or horsehair. It was, perhaps, the head-dress most of all which identified the wearer with a particular region or even with a particular village and it was the one item which seldom changed and whose use survived when all else had been abandoned. A mid-nineteenth-century headscarf (EG 120 1987) from Hungary is illustrated and two different types of cap (EG 1569 and 1583).

LEATHERWORK

In Hungary, famed for its leatherwork, three main types of garment were made, the details and decoration of which varied from area to area. The *suba*, a full-length circular cloak, was worn by men of considerable status in their locality – perhaps members of the village or parish council – while women wore a hip-length version. The *kődmőn* is a jacket worn by men and married women; together with a cow or a calf it often formed the dowry

given to a girl by her father. Men and women also wore a sleeveless waistcoat which was generally not considered important enough to decorate except in Transylvania (Romania) and in some villages in the north, both areas where the *suba* and the *kődmőn* were not common.

Leather appliqué was the only form of decoration until the beginning of the nineteenth century, when silk embroidery became popular, first accompanying appliqué and then often supplanting it. Hungarian sheep produced skins suitable for garments, but not wool suitable for spinning into embroidery threads and it was only after the introduction of Spanish breeds in the nineteenth century that better-quality wool was available. Towards the end of the century this replaced silk for embroidery on leather, being cheaper to buy and quicker to work. The late-nineteenth-century waistcoat on page 143 (EG 286 1983) has wool embroidery as well as leather appliqué.

With local variations, these leather garments were decorated with a wealth of floral motifs which included

recognisable blossoms as well as more stylised ones. Roses, tulips and pomegranates were great sources of inspiration, all three having been introduced by the Ottoman Turks. Pattern books have survived from the beginning of the nineteenth century containing delicate designs of floral sprays, in baskets, or bound by ribbons into bouquets, or growing in pots. Relatively restrained designs from the first half of the nineteenth century became increasingly lavish and by the 1870s many garments were covered with dense and colourful embroidery, gaining in visual impact what was lost in fine detail. In the following decade bourgeois taste began to influence the towns of the Great Plain, rejecting bright colours and crowded designs. These survived, however, in more remote areas well into the twentieth century.

Similar designs were also embroidered by craftsmen on to a more common garment, the *szűr* – a sleeved coat for men made from coarse Hungarian wool and worn like a cloak over the shoulders. Like the leather garments, decoration was originally in the form of appliqué. The earliest references to embroidered *szűr* dates from the first decades of the nineteenth century but it did not become the general fashion until the middle of the century. It was a popular and functional garment, essential for shepherds and herdsmen who spent most of their time outdoors. It

was said that a boy became a 'young man' when he acquired his first *szűr* and he was not allowed to pay court to a girl until he had done so. The cost of a highly decorated one for Sundays and feastdays might be more than a whole year's wage, so men would often resort to stealing horses in order to pay for them. Consequently, several laws were passed in an attempt to prohibit the manufacture of over-adorned *szűr* and their sale to herdsmen and agricultural labourers. Policemen were even empowered to cut the embroidery off over-elaborate garments but it deterred neither the craftsmen nor the customers, and ornate *szűr*s remained popular and precious. Being a particularly Hungarian garment, the *szűr* was used as a declaration of Hungarian patriotism after the failed War of Independence (1848), and was worn by some to demonstrate against the Hapsburgs.

It often happened that expensive items made by professional craftspeople were owned by the village and not by individual families. This custom is understandable with something like the gold metal bridal crown from the Egerland region of Bohemia, but the fact that the bridal blouse was owned in the same way in many villages in Dalmatia and that an embroidered wedding banner was lent out by the villages of western Moravia and south-east Bohemia emphasises the importance of using the correct embroideries at important occasions.

(*left, above*)

Cap, Hungarian or Czechoslovakian, nineteenth century.
In cotton edged with bobbin lace, this is embroidered with very finely spun wool and cotton in shades of red and green, and black and orange. The bands of geometric patterns are worked in a variety of counted-thread stitches and the central band is of pulled thread work
EG 1583, 28 × 32cm (11 × 12½in)

(*left, below*)

Cap, north Hungary or south Slovakia, nineteenth century. Linen decorated with eyelet work is embroidered with yellow silk in stem, satin and double running stitches. This cap would have been gathered to the back through the loops which run along the sides. The inclusion of fine blue threads among the yellow indicates that the cap is from Moravia
EG 1569, 40.5 × 47.5cm (1ft 3¾in × 1ft 6½in)

CHAPTER 6

SYMBOLISM AND STATUS

Costumes and Textiles from China and Japan

Meg Andrews

CHINA

N O PRIOR KNOWLEDGE of Chinese court costumes is necessary to appreciate the rich visual display the Embroiderers' Guild Collection offers, with its variety of stitch techniques (many exclusively Chinese), vibrant exciting colours and interesting subject matter.

Chinese court costumes give a fascinating glimpse into a unique world, where the Emperor was regarded as the son of heaven with mystic powers, and where ceremony and protocol required a great variety of costume, the use of which was governed by law. The complex symbolic decoration of the costume conveyed sophisticated sociological and religious messages to those initiated in court life.

In China, decorated costume and textiles functioned on an intellectual as well as a visual level, and they were considered a major art form, not merely decorative objects. There are good examples of both costumes and textiles in the Embroiderers' Guild Collection and the embroiderer will immediately recognise the quality of workmanship and materials. A fuller appreciation comes with a little knowledge of the social context.

The decoration of most Chinese costumes and textiles is symbolic. Some of the symbols used are related directly to religion and philosophy, whilst others have secular meanings.

DRAGON ROBES

The Ming dynasty established in 1368 was gradually conquered by a minority race, the Manchus from north-east China, who had a highly organised tribal system. The Ming rulers had luxurious sedate lives, a lifestyle reflected in their huge red robes of up to 12 metres (13 yards) of silk, which had sleeves almost to the ground, making movement slow and difficult. The Manchus were a nomadic people, descendants of hunting, fishing and stockbreeding forest tribes who had supplied the Mings with furs, horses and ginseng. When the Manchus came to power they were anxious to reinforce and maintain their ethnic identity, so they introduced a hybrid costume for court wear based on the shape of their traditional costume, developed to suit their nomadic horseriding life. This had originally been based on animal skins, but incorporated the Han Chinese cloth-weaving traditions. (The Han dynasty had been in power during the years 206 BC–AD 220 but its traditions persisted and members of the dynasty continued to play a part in courtly life.)

When the Manchus had been warring nomads they had worn a short jacket and trousers, putting a pleated skirt over the latter for more formal occasions. This tradition continued after they had established themselves in power but the jacket and skirt were combined to form a robe, as in the formal court robes (*chaofu*), worn only at the most important functions, and the dragon robes or mandarin robes (*longpao*), worn for the many semi-formal events by Manchu and Han men and Manchu women.

The Guild has three men's dragon robes, one completely couched in gold- and silver-wrapped silk, another of woven brocade, and the third, an embroidered example, illustrated on page 163 (EG 343). The robes had a curved side-of-chest fastening (based on the outline of an animal skin) and an inner flap which covered half of the front of the jacket, to give protection against the elements – as did the horseshoe cuffs which covered the hands. These were retained on the court robes because the Chinese felt it disrespectful to show their hands. The middle sleeve of plain black or very dark-indigo silk with horizontal bands like tucks – enabling the sleeve to be pushed up the arm with ease – was another feature retained from the nomads' earlier dress, as was the toggle and loop which is the oldest type of fastening. The dragon robe also had a central front and back slit to facilitate walking, another feature developed from horseriding days. The basic shape of the robes did not change for the 268 (1644–1912) years that the Manchus were in power.

The dragon robe was designed to symbolise the concept of universal order, the most important idea in Chinese philosophy, and also to display rank, status and wealth. Only those in court circles could read all the complex messages included. The symbolism was complete only when the robe was worn. The human body became the world axis, with the neck as the gate to heaven or the apex of the universe, separating the material world (the robe) from the spiritual world (the head).

In the nineteenth-century robe illustrated, we see a full-faced dragon (the Emperor) with overlapping scales, which are achieved by layering the couched gold-wrapped silk. (Gold was associated with immortality because of its durability and constancy under changing conditions.) He coils and twists and tries to grasp the flaming pearl (wisdom) with his five claws. By the nineteenth century, five claws did not denote an imperial robe as so often is thought, for, with the dynasty in decline, any person could have five claws embroidered on their robe. He is seen in a cloud-filled sky above a basket of peaches and flowers (Taoist symbol) worked in loose Peking knots. Red bats (good fortune) fly amongst crane medallions (longevity) and other Taoist symbols such as a pair of castanets, a fan, a tube and rods, all embroidered in long and short and surface satin stitch in polychrome floss silks. Below this is a further pair of dragons in profile and a *lishui* (standing-water) border (seas of the world) filled with a *ruyi sceptre* (longevity and good luck), the sacred wheel (a Buddhist symbol), and a pair of gold *fang sheng* rectangular and square ornaments (wealth and fortune). Three mountains (the earth) emerge from the sea at the centre front and back, and are also just visible at the sides of the robe, embroidered in five shades of blue, green and four shades of yellow. Two further dragons are visible on the shoulders of the garment.

The robe has a total of nine main dragons, so it must have belonged to a high ranking official; an unseen dragon is embroidered on an inner flap which covers half of the front of the robe. There are also further smaller dragons on the neck border, and one each on the horseshoe cuffs. The robe's outer edge is made from strips of paper stamped with gold leaf and woven with silk and there are five decorative gilt buttons. The horseshoe cuffs on this robe are poorly couched as is so often the case. Perhaps it was felt the cuff at the end of the long sleeve would not be noticed. The robe has the usual central front and back slit.

Dragon robes can partly be dated by the size of the main chest dragons, the stiffness and rigidity of the decoration and length of the *lishui* border, which became deeper as the nineteenth century progressed. By the time the Guild robe illustrated was made the water is deep and straight and the waves are stiff, whereas the earlier robes have rippling water with undulating waves.

WAISTCOATS

Waistcoats were worn by men or women, either front-flap or side fastening, over informal robes, the armholes cut very wide to accommodate the bulky material of the robe underneath. The Guild's adolescent's waistcoat in silk damask (EG 4497) is delightfully naïve in its design although the quality of the embroidery is very good. It is almost entirely worked in fine Peking knots in pastel shades, with laid floss silks emphasising the features. The front depicts a gardener, and a boy holding a rope jumping off a rock; the reverse side has a central butterfly below lotus and stylised flowers with caterpillars. The edging braid is hand-woven brocade with butterflies and flowers with a similar wider band of shaded blue and white flowers and precious objects, the outer edge being black satin. The gold buttons are engraved with a flower.

Peking knots, which give a flat concentration of colour, resemble French knots but have only one twist which is pulled tightly round the needle as it is worked. The knots are usually worked in groups to give texture and definition. This stitch is commonly called 'forbidden stitch' because it was worked in the workshops of the Forbidden City. It caused great strain on embroiderers' eyes.

RANK BADGES

The practice of wearing rank badges (*puzi*) began during the Yuan Mongol dynasty (1260–1368) and during the Ming period pairs of birds or animals were depicted on badges. There were nine ranks in the Chinese court, divided into military and civil, with the former wearing an animal badge and the latter, which were more highly regarded, a bird, perhaps due to its ability to fly nearer to heaven. During the Qing period the Emperor and Princes wore circular badges with dragons, one back and front and one on each shoulder, the shape associated with heaven and the wearers being considered above earthly spheres. All others wore two badges, one front and one back. Male members of the imperial family wore two circular dragon badges, unrelated nobles wore two square badges, whilst all others wore two squares.

The badge was applied to, or woven into, the mandarin's plain three-quarter length surcoat (*pufu*) and represented the universe. The animal or bird represents the court official, who could be a Manchu or a Han Chinese, always looking at the sun (the Emperor). He stands on the rocks of the earth above the seas of the world surrounded by the sky filled with Buddhist, Taoist or precious objects. The bird on a man's front badge faces his right shoulder and on his back his left.

The badge in the illustration is that of a first-ranking military officer. It shows an animal called a *qilin*, repre-

senting the officer, standing proudly on a rocky outcrop looking at the sun (the Emperor). The cloud-strewn sky has five bats (blessings) holding swastikas (good luck) hovering above a *lishui* border, the border having *xi* (joy) and *shou* (longevity) symbols. The *qilin* was considered auspicious and the noblest of creatures, having the body of a deer, the tail of an ox and the hooves of a horse. When it walked it did not crush the grass and ate no living creature, sparing the innocent, but it struck the guilty with its single horn, its actions determined by the judge Gaoyao. The five bats depict the five blessings – long life, riches, virtue, health and natural death. Bats are symbols of happiness and good luck.

The badge is beautifully embroidered with silver-gilt-wrapped silk, with a thicker thread outlining each scale to give definition, the gold caught down with yellow and the silver with white silk. The tumbling waves are also couched and caught down with blue, green and mauve in slightly thicker thread to emphasise the colour. Long and short, stem and surface satin stitch have also been used in two thicknesses of polychrome floss silks. The sun is of small coral beads and the background of black satin.

(*previous page and left*)
HAN CHINESE adolescent's waistcoat and an insignia, or badge of rank (*puzi*), Chinese, last quarter of the nineteenth century (details from both shown here in black and white).

The waistcoat is almost entirely worked in fine Peking knots with laid floss. The front shows a gardener with a perplexed look on his face with a large butterfly hovering above.

The badge is of a first-ranking military officer with a *qilin* (official) standing proudly on a rocky outcrop. Black satin is embroidered with silver-gilt-wrapped silk. Long and short stitches, stem and surface satin stitch have been used in two thicknesses of polychrome floss silks

Waistcoat: EG 4497, length 44cm (1ft 5in). Given by Mrs W. J. Roberts. Badge: EG 20 1990, width 31 × 32cm (1ft × 1ft ½in)

Floss silk was made from the soft external covering of silkworm cocoons and is an untwisted yarn which can be split down into five threads. Other badges in the collection are worked with floss, twisted silks or gold wrapped round a silk core for couching. Stitches used are Peking knots, tent and counted stitching, couching in metallic threads, or a combination of stitches. One military badge depicting a panther, worn by a sixth-degree official, has the couched gold and silver animal appliquéd to the ground. This is typical of many of the insignia dating from *c*1900 where one sees the bird crudely tacked to the ground fabric or where there is just a blank unembroidered space for the motif. Purchasing the civil service examination results was quite common by the 1770s but during the second half of the nineteenth century, when China was in decline and standards slipped even further, it was even easier to buy your way to the next rank, with price lists being issued during the later part of the nineteenth century. To save the expense of buying a completely new badge with each promotion, badges were made so that the bird or animal could be easily taken off and the next rank applied. Many of these badges have bright colouring or are completely couched with gold- and silver-wrapped silk. Most of these would

MANCHU LADY'S informal robe (*changfu*), Chinese, late nineteenth century. Red satin is embroidered in polychrome floss silks mainly in satin stitch. The sleevebands of cream satin are finely worked with pastel-shaded flowers. The robe appears never to have been finished as it is unlined and the sleeve bands have only been tacked in
EG 5649, length 140cm (4ft 6½in). Given by Mrs J. Pritchard

SEMI-FORMAL man's dragon robe (*longpao*), Chinese, last quarter of the nineteenth century.
Blue silk twill is embroidered with nine dragons. Red bats fly amongst crane medallions above a standing-wave (*lishui*) border. The full-faced dragon (the Emperor) has overlapping scales achieved by layering the couched gold-wrapped silk. The robe would have been worn in spring for semi-formal routine court occasions by a high ranking mandarin
EG 343, length 143cm (4ft 7¾in). Given by Mrs Thomas Wood

have been made by men and boys in professional workshops, although occasionally they would have been worked at home.

The gold-wrapped silk used for couching and weaving was used in both China and Japan. Gold was hammered and beaten into small squares, laid side by side on very fine paper for further beating, to produce a long band which was then cut into very fine strips with an incredibly heavy axe-like tool. The gold was then hand spun round the silk core and stored on a spool.

Women wore the badge of their husband, son or father depending on their status, wearing the badge in reverse with the animal or bird facing the opposite direction. Manchu ladies wore theirs on their calf-length surcoats, whilst Han Chinese wore theirs on sleeveless tasselled tabards over short or three-quarter-length robes, skirts and trousers.

OTHER ACCESSORIES

Over formal court robes (*chaofu*) as well as semi-formal surcoats (*pufu*) wide flaring *piling* collars, which probably derived from hoods, were worn by both men and women. The Guild's example (EG 3873), not illustrated, of twill silk is quite finely embroidered with startled-looking dragons chasing flaming pearls, couched with gold-wrapped silk held down by red silks and embroidered with pale blue, ivory, purple and dark green floss silks, the border of extended blue and green clouds alternating with nine bats.

To complete these outfits black satin boots with rigid layered cotton and leather stitched soles were worn.

WOMEN'S INFORMAL WEAR

There are many informal Manchu women's robes (*changpao*) in the Collection, long and three-quarter length, front or side fastening – with these the women could express some choice. These robes were of plain silk, silk damask, velvet, satin or *kesi* (silk woven on a loom in the tapestry technique), with edgings and sleeve bands. They were decorated with beautiful symbolic flowers, insects and birds, and were bulky and flowing as to reveal the figure would have been thought offensive. Robes were never hung but laid in camphor or sandalwood chests to deter mites.

The best example in the Collection (EG 5649) is in red satin and would have been worn in the spring. It is finely embroidered in polychrome floss silks mainly in satin stitch. The design has large hydrangea heads, with shaded pale green, apricot and ivory flowers, between small sprays of chrysanthemums (symbol of autumn), peonies (spring) and magnolia (the spring welcoming

flower but also meaning a beautiful woman). The neck and hem band of ivory satin are embroidered with butterflies (joy) flitting amongst daisies, chrysanthemums, peonies, prunus (winter) and narcissus (a New Year plant and one of good fortune). The sleevebands are of cream satin finely worked with pastel-shaded flowers.

The robe appears never to have been finished as it is unlined and the sleevebands have only been tacked in. It is interesting to observe the seams, which have had paste applied to them, as was common with Chinese garments, and are therefore quite crisp. The robe was then crudely sewn together with large back stitches, which again is quite normal.

Han women took no part in court proceedings and therefore their costume was not regulated. Their robes tended to be short or three-quarter length, side fastening, similar to the Manchus' but, often with more widely cut body and sleeves, in the Old Ming style, which only they were allowed to wear. The Guild has an example in midblue silk damask (EG 2780, not illustrated), widely cut with a variety of flower sprigs, the sleevebands of very fine-quality embroidery with pinky-red peonies emerging from archaic vessels and an inner border of flowers on a gold and black swastika ground.

SLEEVEBANDS

Sleevebands tend to have plain fronts and embroidered backs; the reasoning is not clear until the arms are folded in front, with the back section of the band on view. Sleevebands are a good source for stitches and inspiration as well as showing qualities of workmanship and subject matter. Some are completely horizontally couched, some are entirely in tent stitch, others are in Peking knots; some are completely outlined in couched gold-wrapped silk.

There are many lovely sleevebands in the Collection. The finest pair, in silk damask gauze, is embroidered in clear polychrome shades. The detail illustrated (EG 1073) shows a dragon boat full of oarsmen with a boy standing astride the dragon's head waving a flag (the dragon's scales outlined with couched gold-wrapped silk), below a bridge worked in laid silks with an overlay of star stitch, to give the effect of a trellis. Note the people on the bridge, with the mandarin who has couched gold glasses, the lady with the fan and the man with the pipe. Radiating satin stitches are also used for the pine trees' foliage.

Another pair celebrating the same event, the Dragon Boat Festival, should be mentioned. Not nearly of such fine quality or interesting stitches, they do have iridescent peacock feathers couched on to them to resemble lichen.

The Dragon Boat Festival is celebrated on the fifth day of the fifth moon in central and southern China. The

SLEEVEBAND (detail), from a pair belonging to a lady's robe, celebrating the Dragon Boat Festival, Chinese, last quarter of the nineteenth century. The detail shows a dragon boat full of oarsmen with a boy standing astride the dragon's head waving a flag. The dragon's scales are outlined with couched gold-wrapped silk. The bridge is worked in laid silks with an overlay of star stitch to give the effect of trellis *EG 1073, 48.5 × 14cm (1ft 7in × 5½in). Given by Miss H. G. Ionides*

(above)

A HAN LADY'S apron or skirt and a marriage overskirt, last quarter of the nineteenth century.

(left) A very fine quality skirt of silk damask gauze embroidered with two panels of butterflies and peonies worked in block satin stitch with voiding. The pleated side sections, similarly worked, have straight stitch and Peking knots.

(right) Marriage skirt with central front and back panel, flanked by narrow lappets, embroidered with a dragon and a phoenix, the rocks couched with gold-wrapped silk. The flowers in polychrome silks are in long and short, and stem stitch
Apron: EG 36, length 94cm (3ft ½in). Marriage skirt (right): EG 3376, length 100cm (3ft 3in). Both given by Queen Mary

(right)

M AN'S GIRDLE SET which would have been worn hanging from a belt in the third quarter of the nineteenth century.

The little pouches were made to be 'read': the swastikas read as *wan* or 10,000, and the bats read as *fu*, a pun for blessings, together meaning 10,000 blessings. They were made in red silk, now faded to terracotta, with a swastika fretwork ground worked in rare Pekinese stitch. The swastikas are made of silver-wrapped silk forming loops with back stitch in ivory silk. The bats are worked in twisted silk cords in shades of apricot, red, green, blue, purple, black and ivory. The work is exceptionally fine. All have ochre silk drawstrings with silver decorative endless knots, or bindings of ochre silk. The set comprises (from centre left clockwise) a watch case, tobacco pouch, spectacle case, calling card case, fan case, and (centre) two heart-shaped pouches, one of which still has the cottonwool which would have been impregnated with scent
EG 94, fan case 32cm (1ft ½in) long. Given by Mrs Nicholson

Festival is believed to be in memory of Qu Yuan who drowned himself in 295 BC after having been falsely accused of a crime. The people, believing him, prepared rice cakes and set out with gongs and flags in boats to make sacrifices, and this has been celebrated as an annual holiday ever since.

Another band, completely worked in counted stitch on a silk gauze ground, has children on sampans, and people fishing. Another, with small children (one carrying a *juji* sceptre) is worked with pineneedle, netting and stem stitch. There is also a pair worked entirely in Peking knot with birds, and frogs perched on rocks; these are unfinished and one can see the ink drawing. On them the trees sprout peonies and gourds, the latter being given a two-tone effect by the use of green and yellow silks mixed, whilst the peonies are worked in five shades of red silk. One pair has goldfish swimming amongst lotus, another has warriors on horseback.

SKIRTS

There are eighteen skirts, or aprons as they are called, in the Collection, all of which would have been worn with a short or three-quarter-length robe, either front or side fastening, by Han ladies. Under the skirts, trousers would have been worn, as they had been since the second century BC. All these skirts are of satin or silk; one is padded for winter wear and others are of silk gauze for summer.

Chinese skirts are usually made in either two unjoined sections attached at the top of each section by a wide cotton waistband, or they have a common cotton waistband. Each section has two central panels, to wear centre back and front, each panel flanked on one side by either honeycomb or ordinary pleating or straight gores. The embroidery was only worked on the lower part of the skirt, the part which showed beneath the robe.

Queen Mary gave the Guild two very fine skirts, illustrated. One (EG 36) of silk damask gauze in eggyolk yellow embroidered with two panels of eight butterflies flitting amongst peonies. The blue floss silk peonies and prunus are worked in block satin stitch with voiding (unworked space between the embroidery). The beautiful butterflies, each quite different, are in mauve, purple, green, brown, black and ivory silks. This theme of butterflies and peonies is a recurring one in Chinese embroideries. The butterfly was a symbol of longevity and the peony was the flower of riches and honour, both age and wealth being highly respected. It was also said that when peonies and butterflies were depicted together it symbolised a young girl (the former) attracting a young man (the latter). The pleated side sections are embroidered with narcissus flowers and the various-width braids similarly worked. Other stitches worked on the

skirt are straight and Peking knots.

There are various methods of pleating skirts. One method is to draw vertical lines on both sides of the fabric. The cloth is then folded on the lines and each end of the cloth is firmly stitched. The fabric is then tied over a long half-section of bamboo tube, inserted into a larger bamboo tube and steamed for an hour. The cloth is removed, allowed to dry and is then ready for use.

BRIDAL WEAR

Marriage skirts were also worn only by the Han population and the illustrated example (EG 3376) is typical. It is formed of a central front and back panel flanked by narrower lappets, all attached at the top to a cotton waistband. As none of these were joined together, some type of underskirt would have been worn. This is a very fine piece with its central front and back satin panels each embroidered with a dragon and a phoenix, the latter with neck feathers in alternate silks of black and beige in straight stitch, the rocks couched with gold-wrapped silk. Both panels are edged with macramé-plaited silks, endless knots and tassels. The lappets of yellow, apricot, rust, blue and green satin are all beautifully embroidered in polychrome floss silks with butterflies, prunus, chrysanthemums, narcissus, lotus flowers and peaches, in long and short stem stitches. All the panels are edged with fine, narrow, hand-woven brocade braid and the whole is lined with pale apricot silk damask.

Red, the colour of happiness, was the customary colour for bridal robes, wedding hangings and altar cloths, and for any joyful occasion such as birth. At weddings the bride and groom were considered to be the Emperor and Empress for the day. Because the phoenix was the ruler of the birds and representative of the Empress, and the dragon ruler of the animals and representative of the Emperor, the couple were entitled to have this pair embroidered on their wedding robes.

An interesting bridal cloud collar (*yun chien*) in the Collection, again worn only by Han ladies, was another item of clothing having cosmic symbolism when worn (not illustrated). It is shaped like a square yoke but has points hanging down the front, back and shoulders, to mark the cardinal points surrounding the wearer's head. Each section is embroidered with ladies and boys, bordered with hand-made braids in varying widths, and has mid-blue silk stitching, decorative knotting and long tassels.

The fine silk garments forming part of a Han bride's trousseau had the cut of ancient Chinese court robes, very full and with wide sleeves. These robes were part of the wealth women brought to a family and it was in her role as bride that a woman obtained any status or social prominence. The status of well-off families was enhanced if the woman was a good embroideress, whereas in a poor family such skills helped with the income.

There is a very bright Han wedding robe in the Collection (EG 3376), not illustrated, cut in the ancient court style, of pillarbox red satin and crudely but effectively couched and embroidered with a dragon chasing the flaming pearl. Its body is worked in heavy gold thread with loose floss silks used in bright shades of emerald, royal and pale blue, and its nose and flaming pearl are in loose Peking knots. Below it is a pavilion flanked by a pair of phoenix and dragons emerging from clouds, with bats and baskets surrounding them. The *lishui* border is striped with nine lines of couched threads and has a pair of *qilin* (mythical beasts) playing with a ball. The wide sleeves have dragons similar to the others on the robe, surrounded by five bats.

SHOES

In John Thompson's book of photographs on China first published in 1873 he states: Girls were betrothed at around 14 years of age and a girl from a wealthy family would have been required to have some 30 pairs of shoes for her marriage trousseau alone. During negotiations the girl's shoes were shown to the prospective family to be inspected for size and quality of embroidery. Many women would embroider their own shoes, although many also bought them.

Han women bound their feet since the Song dynasty (AD 960–1279) and the custom probably originated from some primitive tribal custom instituted to prevent women from straying from their immediate boundaries. Sex segregation increased during the Song dynasty and the practice of foot binding became widespread. Bound feet were not only considered feminine and seductive and associated with physical delicacy, but also became a symbol of caste, for the peasant classes could not afford to immobilise its women. Deformed and crippled feet became symbols to enhance the status of men as providers. In pretty shoes with pantaloons falling over the swollen and deformed ankles the girl hobbled along on the arm of a servant. If any distance had to be covered, a sedan chair would have been used. Girls' feet were bound at around four years of age, the tight bandages never being permanently removed. The mission schools refused to take girls with bound feet in an attempt to stop the practice. In 1911 a law was passed abolishing the custom. Before that women in some cities had discontinued the practice but in country districts it lingered for some time. Bound-feet shoes were presented by women to the goddess Guanyin to encourage her to endow them with children.

People are fascinated, as well as repelled, by this custom but unfortunately there is only one pair of shoes for bound feet in the Collection (EG 35). The shoes have the central front of ivory silk damask embroidered with radiating pineneedle stitch, stem and satin stitch. The sides are of indigo satin with gold- and silver-wrapped silk, couched with red and white silks respectively, with a peony and trailing buds. Each section is divided by narrow hand-made braids and cord. The shaped heel is 2.3cm (15/16in) high and covered with pale yellow silk with a turquoise flower edged in black, purple, blue or ivory rouleau silk. The curved sole of turquoise cotton is padded and stitched with a white silk flower, beautifully and minutely worked. When the lady was sitting cross legged the soles would of course be seen. The back of each shoe has a pink cotton tab crudely stitched to the shoe, with orange looped cords. This enabled the wearer to pull on the shoe, the tab then being tucked into the shoe out of sight. The shoes are lined in natural cotton.

BAGS AND POUCHES

During the Han dynasty nomads migrating into central China wore leather belts with decorative inlays and small hanging leather strips to which they attached items to be used in everyday life including probably food. This form of belt became popular with the civilian population including women and became one of 'the seven necessities', others being fire, stone, tinder set, flint, knife and needle. Gradually lettercases, money packet and mirror bag replaced the seven necessities for men, and women wore small hanging gadgets and brocade bags stuffed with incense or filled with jewels and curios, worn for decorative purposes only.

During the Qing dynasty (1644–1911 BC) when laws governing dress were implemented, belts were of silk fabric, with different colours representing different ranks. The belts had decorative metal or gold clasps inlaid with jade and metal rings from which to hang purses. They might carry a purse for incense, fan, eyeglass, knife, money, watch, earpicks, sweetmeats, rings, chopsticks and cutlery.

Women's robes were not belted so they were not able to carry personal items. They did, however, hang incense bags and manicure tools from a lapel button or from the fastening at the side of their robes and also hid small bags and fan cases up their large sleeves.

Small bags were also used in the bedchamber, filled with perfume and hung from the bedcurtains.

On New Year's Eve, the Emperor would give purses embroidered by the court ladies to his esteemed officials and servants together with a small gift such as a gold or silver charm. Should the Emperor bestow his own purse

Man's tobacco pouch and a pouch for gaming discs, both Chinese, late nineteenth century.

The oblong pouch for gaming discs is in black satin; the snarling dragons have claws sparred, their bodies worked in Pekinese stitch with eyes of knots. The clouds and wave border at the base are all in silver- and gold-wrapped silk, couched and highlighted with pink and purple and shades of blue and yellow silk and edged with hand-made braid in two shades of blue with additional silver thread. The sides are couched with *shou* (longevity) and *xi* (joy) symbols. The inner box of bright yellow satin opens to reveal a red satin interior with divisions. The cords attached to the top of the reticule are beautifully made and have decorative abacus knots above bound tassels
EG 2, length 12cm (4¾in)

The other pouch of silk gauze shaped like a gourd (the symbol of medication) was used for tobacco which was thought to be a healing drug and was commonly used by both men and women, and not only for medicinal purposes! The pouch, worked entirely in diagonal tent stitch, depicts a fisherman carrying a large net beneath a cluster of houses and a pagoda, set amongst trees and with mountains in the distance. The reverse side has a similar scene but a man is now sitting in a junk with temples, houses, a bridge and a pagoda in the distance. All is in shades of red, blue, black, ochre, apricot and four shades of green, two of lilac pink, and taupe silks, edged in a black and ivory hand-woven silk braid. At strategic places, where the pouch bears the strain of being opened, the edge is strengthened with oversewing of black satin
EG 94, 18 × 9cm (7 × 3½in)

(right)
A pair of Han Chinese lady's shoes for bound feet, late nineteenth century.
The shoes, only 11cm (4¼in) long, have a central front of ivory silk damask embroidered with radiating pineneedle stitch, stem and satin stitch. The sides are embroidered with gold- and silver-wrapped silk, couched with red and white silks. The curved sole of cotton is padded and stitched
EG 35, length 11cm (4¼in). Given by Lady Reynolds Stephens

IDOL'S CAPE AND HOOD, Chinese, eighteenth century. These very small garments are of imperial yellow satin, embroidered in satin stitch with couching, have a central dragon chasing the flaming pearl and flanked by a pair of side-facing dragons, all above a standing-wave (*lishui*) border, the sky with clouds and bat. The cape is split up the back and strengthened with rows of horizontal stitching. On either side of the split is calligraphy which translates 'In illustrious memory'. The peaked hood also has a pair of facing dragons. There is some calligraphy in black silks which reads 'From the hall of the three virtues, with a guileless heart to end the suppression of righteousness' *EG 154, cape 26cm (10in) long. Given by Queen Mary (Photograph: Dudley Moss)*

to a subject or visitor, this was an honour indeed. In his book *Embassy to China*, published in 1797, Sir George Staunton relates how a thirteen-year-old boy, the only member of the British Ambassador's party to speak Chinese, was given one for acting as interpreter.

Women and girls would make and embroider these purses at home. Children would be given them at special celebrations and for their birthdays or at New Year, when a popular snack such as toasted beans wrapped in red paper was enclosed. The bags had different shapes and were considered lucky and able to protect from smallpox. A bride would also present little pouches she had embroidered to her older female relatives, and in particular her mother-in-law.

EMBROIDERIES FOR IDOLS

One of the finest and oldest pieces in the Collection is a small eighteenth-century idol's cape and hood of imperial yellow satin (EG 154). It is embroidered with a central dragon chasing a flaming pearl, flanked by a pair of side-facing dragons. A *lishui* border and sky with clouds and bats completes the design. The cape is split up the back and strengthened with rows of horizontal stitching, rather like the pouches. On either side of the split is some calligraphy which translates 'In illustrious memory'. The peaked hood also has a pair of facing dragons. There is some calligraphy in black silks which translates 'From the hall of the three virtues, with a guileless heart to end the suppression of righteousness'.

A little circular embroidery in the Collection (EG 1548), not illustrated, which resembles a collar, may well have been made for an idol. It is beautifully worked in four sections, each containing scrolls, a box or game and a lute. The scrolls are worked in pink and green floss silks and most of the sections are worked in minute needle darning, which resembles weaving, in six different patterns, all outlined in couched gold- or silver-wrapped silk. The lute is worked with laid brown silks over which ivory silks in a diamond pattern are couched. Another section has a cord worked with overcast stitch to emphasise it. Narrow hand-made braids divide the section and the neck opening. The outer edge has plaited gold-wrapped thread and a wide outer band of blue satin.

HANGINGS

There are many large embroidered hangings in the Collection. These were used as altar cloths (most houses had a small altar), wall coverings, bedcurtains and banners, or for export. High-quality tribute hangings were also made.

One of the most spectacular in the Collection is a piece made in Hong Kong by the Chinese community for Sir Henry Francis May KCMG, a respected figure, Colonial Secretary of Hong Kong and Governor Designate of Fiji in 1911 (see page 174). It was presented to him on his departure from Hong Kong. The top section of this hanging has four bold calligraphy characters above Confucius seated at a table surrounded by four of his followers, their robes shimmering with two shades of floss silk. The figures are on a prunus-garlanded terrace with bamboo, willow and chrysanthemum bushes, all above a central field covered with calligraphy – the names of the men who gave the address to Sir Henry about his career – flanked by borders, each with four of the 'Eight Immortals' between peony, chrysanthemum and lotus flowers. The Eight Immortals, six men and two women, each represented a different condition in life, eg poverty, wealth, aristocracy, masculinity and femininity. They achieved immortality by their good works. Their attributes symbolised the successful search for everlasting life and became associated with wishes for good fortune.

The base of the hanging has a further panel showing the Emperor resplendent in yellow attended by two soldier brothers. He is inviting his third brother to become a minister. The soldiers' armour is particularly splendid with satin stitches in a shell formation and minute infill satin stitches. Their swords are of laid stitch and their faces made with realistic plastic-composition 'ivory', painted, carved and sewn on, covering faces that have been beautifully embroidered. Even the soles of their boots appear to have been quilted; all this contained between side borders with Peking-knot peaches and flowers in archaic vessels between delicate flower sprays, worked in soft pastel shades. This magnificent embroidery hangs from a thick carved ivory scroll with three-dimensional dragons, and has its own carved wood box on a stand. The box interior is painted with birds and flowers.

Another spectacular hanging (not illustrated) was made for Edward Prince of Wales on his visit to Singapore in 1923, the top embroidered with 'The Kwon Tung Community of Singapore respectfully greets HRH The Prince of Wales'. Of bright red satin, this hanging which measures 1.6 × 0.6m (5ft 4in × 2ft) has scenes from daily court life. This incredibly bright piece has a great variety of stitches and techniques.

The Emperor and Empress are seen holding court, surrounded by courtiers, warlords and dancing girls. Some of the dignitaries have rabbit-fur-edged robes, and armour is represented by horizontal rows of couched silver- or gold-wrapped silk thread caught down at intervals. Strips of silver are laid over rolls of cotton padding, some caught down either side of the roll and some carried across to imitate folds in clothes. The jovial-looking horses are raised and padded and worked in encroaching satin stitch. The dragons on the men's robes are crudely but effectively worked by making the couched gold thread into loops to imitate their scales. Below is a panel of calligraphy contained in medallions with Buddhas, lions, archaic vessels filled with flowers, bronze censers, and a rabbit. Unusually, the maker's name is included.

SILK PRODUCTION AND EMBROIDERY WORKSHOPS

The Chinese were the first people to weave silk from the *Bombyx mori*, the silkworm moth, with production becoming widespread by the Shang and Zhou dynasties (*c*1700–1027 BC and *c*1027–771 BC). The Romans thought that silk was a type of vegetable fibre which grew on trees and it was not until the mid-sixteenth century that the secret was finally smuggled out of China. China had been exporting silk to the Middle East across a caravan trail, later the Silk Road, since the middle of the Zhou dynasty and figured silks have been found in tombs of this period.

In early centuries a good 'harvest' of silk became almost as important as a good grain harvest. Raising silkworms was an extremely demanding task that filled a period from twenty-three to about forty days between the hatching of the larvae to the spinning of the cocoons. The newly hatched silkworm larvae had to be placed in baskets and fed three times daily with finely shredded mulberry leaves. As the worms underwent their first moulting period, they were transferred to shallow bamboo trays, and as they went through the three moulting stages the feeding had to be adjusted. To avoid diseases it was important that the silkworms be kept from dark and damp places; should the weather turn chilly it was necessary to warm the silkworm room with lamps and braziers. At this stage almost the entire family would be toiling day and night, until the silkworms were mature enough to be placed on the strawcocks where the cocoons were made.

The silkworms finally spun their cocoons of fine thread which were sent to a filature where they were boiled to dissolve the sticky substance (sericin) which surrounds the thread. The long, fine, continuous fibre was then unreeled in one continuous length, ready for dyeing or weaving.

By the Ming dynasty (1368–1643) silk was plentiful and fairly cheap and merchants, scholars and nobles used it in their homes for decorative purposes, as well as for their personal adornment. Vast quantities of silk were collected in taxes whilst emperors gave bolts of silk as gifts to foreign emissaries and as tokens of favour to faithful subjects, and it became a medium of exchange.

Thousands of workers were employed in the imperial workshops, where women and girls would embroider the accessories and the lighter summer gauze robes, whilst men would work the heavier robes and hangings. Apart from these there were thousands of workshops set up, some in people's homes accommodating their household's looms, others in larger premises where people were employed. In the nineteenth century a skilled embroiderer earned more than a silversmith but a quarter of the wages of a first-class ivory carver. In every home embroidery techniques were passed down from mother to daughter, embroidery being the only artistic and creative outlet encouraged by society for women. Needles with round eyes were used, with a needle puller, made of brass or wood, for pulling needles through heavy fabrics. A brass or iron thimble, without the top, was worn upon the second joint of the right middle finger.

The fabric worn was seasonal with men and women wearing the same. In spring a satin or silk robe would have been worn, lined with silk; in summer a robe of unlined silk gauze was worn, with a thin silk or silk gauze robe underneath. For autumn there were silk or satin robes with a padded silk lining made from wild silkworms, and for winter, there were furs. In the coldest months, several layers of thin robes were worn, giving a very bulky look.

JAPAN

There are only a few Japanese embroideries in the Collection but they include a particularly fine kimono which is illustrated. Kimono literally translates as 'the thing worn'. These kimonos always appear to be excessively long but one should remember that they did sweep the ground. Japanese women wore elevated wooden pattens on their feet to give them height and dignity, and an *obi* or sash which would have taken up some of the length of the kimono. The warm, humid climate required a garment which was airy and roomy. The wide-sleeved kimono was suitable for leisured ladies, but not conducive to activity.

The best kimono in the Collection is a furisode (swinging sleeves), a type which has been worn since the seventeenth century and was particularly popular during the late Edo period. The furisode was worn originally by apprentice geishas and unmarried girls under the age of nineteen, but by the nineteenth century it was popular for all fashionable ladies.

EMBROIDERED 'ADDRESS' (with detail) housed in a carved rosewood chest, on a stand, Chinese, 1911.
The 'address' is an embroidered version of the speech of thanks given to Sir Henry Francis May KCMG, Colonial Secretary of Hong Kong, on his departure from Hong Kong to become Governor of Fiji. This detail shows Confucius seated at a table with four of his followers, their robes embroidered in floss silk, and their faces made in imitation ivory
EG 9 1990, chest 115 × 346cm (3ft 9in × 11ft 3in). Given by Major Johnson

ROUNDEL OF BIRDS, Chinese, made in Guangdong, south-east China, for export, c1820–50.
This is beautifully embroidered with eight pairs of birds, including *feng-huang* (a mythical phoenix-type bird), ducks, ravens, magpies (birds of joy), birds of paradise, martins, and one kingfisher, all perching, swimming and flying amongst peonies which, due to the subtle colour variation, appear to be three dimensional. Lotus, narcissus and daisies are worked in fine floss silks in shades of apricot, banana, yellow, ivory, bright China and mid-blue, green, mauve, brown, black and ivory, all on ivory satin, using French knots, long and short stitches, straight satin, stem and back stitches, laidwork and voiding. According to legend the *feng-huang* appears only in times of peace and prosperity and will only rest on the hardest of trees, the *wu t'ung* tree (*Dryandra*) or rest on ground bare of vegetation. A pair of mandarin ducks, thought to mate for life, symbolise devotion, and pairs of birds and butterflies symbolise marital happiness
EG 3899, diameter 36cm (1ft 2in). Given by Queen Mary (Photograph: Dudley Moss)

The pale to mid-blue satin of the furisode on page 178 is scattered with gold-leaf fans, some open and others half closed. Each is outlined with rows of laid gold thread and has exquisite embroidered scenes of people and animals on a sponged gold leaf, speckled, or plain gold, ground. The stitches include satin and long and short stitch, with some areas worked over cord to give a raised effect. Whipped silk cord is additionally used for textured effects. The five flower-shaped medallions are placed directly to the right and left of the front opening and at the centre and on both shoulders on the back.

The detail illustrated shows a courtier on horseback. His robes are worked in satin stitch in a diamond pattern with laid and couched threads, and the horse's mane is quite realistically embroidered.

Other fans on the robe show three minogame (tortoise). Their heads and legs are of French knots, and their bodies are of couched gold thread over cord to give emphasis and an undulating effect. Another fan shows Karako, a Chinese boy who was attached to the Japanese court. His clothes are worked in satin stitch with couching threads down the turquoise robe to emphasise the folds; his dog has real hair whiskers. What appear to be five *mon* or family crests are merely decorative motifs.

Made of straight strips of silks, kimonos were loosely basted together so they could be easily taken apart for cleaning. The opening for the hand is quite small even though the sleeve is large. With both men's and women's kimonos the left side overlaps the right.

The gold-leaf technique, known as *nuihaku*, is worked in the following manner. A stencil for the design is cut in heavyweight oiled paper and a loose paste squeezed over leaving the wet paste design imprinted on the fabric. The stencil is then removed and gold or silver leaf, which comes in thin sheets, is pressed on to the wet paste adhering it to the fabric. The area is then burnished lightly.

There are also several large late-nineteenth-century embroidered Japanese hangings in the Collection. Such hangings were presumably made for the export market as many have appeared in the West. All those in the Collection are predominantly in brown, sepia and beige tones using thick, couched, twisted cord and gold couching, with the background often in coils.

One has a cockerel perched on a drum and in the distance a *Sennin* (immortal) flying on a crane. Couched with heavy twisted cotton and gold and silver-gilt thread, the piece is well worn enabling us to see the paper filling below the embroidery.

Another very unusual hanging (not illustrated) was made in Japan for the Chinese market and has Chinese children playing on a bridge, with a dragon swimming in waves, but with a Japanese lady in the background.

A further example has a huge peacock filling a third of the ground, his feathers spread, some worn to reveal the cottonwool padding, all worked in long floss silks and couched with gold threads. There are many slightly raised peonies with French-knot flower centres, all in blues, grey, brown, beige and autumnal colours.

(right; and detail, left)
LARGE DECORATIVE wallhanging, Japanese, late nineteenth century. This hanging depicts a garden with gates, fences and small birds flying amongst exotic flowers and has a background of couched gold-wrapped silk worked in coils. Floss and twisted silk in long and short stitch, padded satin flowers, French knots and laidwork have all been used. There is also silk cord used for the basketweave effect behind the two small birds in the centre of the hanging and for the water at the front
EG 3830, 400 × 470cm (13ft 1in × 15ft 3¼in) (Photograph: Rose & Dyble)

(*right; and detail, left*)

FURISODE KIMONO (swinging sleeves), Japanese, late Edo period (1615–1868). The pale blue satin is scattered with gold-leaf fans outlined with rows of laid gold thread and embroidered with exquisite scenes in satin, long and short stitches with some areas worked over cord to give a raised effect. The detail shows a courtier on horseback, his robes worked in satin stitch in a chevron pattern with laid and couched threads
EG 20 1984, length 162cm (5ft 3in). Given by Mrs Hamilton Bruce

BIBLIOGRAPHY

CHAPTER 1

Bridgeman, H. and Drury, E. (eds). *Needlework: An Illustrated History* (Paddington Press, 1978)

Clabburn, P. *The Needleworker's Dictionary* (Macmillan, 1976)

Colby, Avril. *Samplers* (Batsford, 1964)

Crompton, R. *Modern Design in Embroidery* (Batsford, 1936)

Cumming, V. *Gloves* (Batsford, 1982)

Edwards, J. *Bead Embroidery* (Batsford, 1966)
  Embroidery (Bayford, 1978)
  Dorothy Benson (Bayford Books, 1989)

Ewles, Rosemary. 'One Thousand Years of History' in *The Royal School of Needlework Book of Needlework and Embroidery* ed Lanto Synge (Collins, 1986)

Hillier, Bevis. *Art Deco* (Studio Vista, 1968)

Houston-Almqvist, J. *Mountmellick Work* (Dryad Press, 1985)

Howard, C. *Twentieth Century Embroidery in Great Britain* 4 volumes (to 1939; 1940–63; 1964–78; 1978–84) (Batsford, 1984)

Humphrey, C. 'Canvas Work' in *The Royal School of Needlework Book of Needlework and Embroidery* ed Lanto Synge (Collins, 1986)

Johnstone, Pauline. *Three Hundred Years of Embroidery 1600–1900* (Wakefield Press, 1986)

King, D. *Samplers* (HMSO, 1960)

Levey, Santina M. *Discovering Embroidery of the Nineteenth Century* (Shire Publications, 1971)
  Lace: A History (Victoria & Albert Museum and W. S. Maney & Son Ltd, 1983)

Morris, Barbara. *Victorian Embroidery* (Herbert Jenkins, 1962)

Parry, L. *Textiles of the Arts and Crafts Movement* (Thames & Hudson, 1986)
  Canvaswork (Unwin Hyman, 1987)
  Patchwork (Unwin Hyman, 1987)

Proctor, M. G. *Victorian Canvas work* (Batsford, 1972)

Reiter Weismann, Judith, and Lavitt, Wendy. *Labors of Love* (Studio Vista, 1987)

Scott-James, Desmond, and Wood *The British Museum Book of Flowers* (1989)

Stewart, Imogen 'Embroidery and Dress' in *The Royal School of Needlework Book of Needlework and Embroidery* ed Lanto Synge (Collins, 1986)

Swain, Margaret. *The Flowerers* (W. & R. Chambers, 1955)

Ayrshire and Other Whitework (Shire Publications Ltd, 1982)

Wingfield-Digby, G. F. *Elizabethan Embroidery* (Faber & Faber, 1963)

CHAPTER 2

Swan, S. B. *Plain and Fancy: American Women and Their Needlework*, 1700–1850 (Holt, Rinehart and Winston, 1977)

CHAPTER 3

Ackerman, P. 'Embroidery in Persia', *Embroidery* (Vol 3 no 1, 1934)

Argenti, Philip. *Costumes of Chios* (Batsford, 1953)

Azak, G., and Koyas, E. F. *On Bin Türk Motifi Ansiklopedisi* (Ten Thousand Turkish Motifs) (1984)

Bent, Theodore. *The Cyclades or Life among the Insular Greeks* (Longmans, Green & Co, 1885)

Berry, Burton Yost. 'Old Turkish Towels II', *The Art Bulletin* (Vol 20, 1938)

Black, David, and Loveless, Clive. *İşlemeler: Ottoman Domestic Embroideries* (David Black Oriental Carpets, 1978)
  Embroidered Flowers from Thrace to Tartary (David Black Oriental Carpets [exhibition catalogue] 1981)

Blunt, Fanny. *The People of Turkey* (2 vols) (John Murray, 1878)

Chardin, Sir John. *Travels in Persia* (Argonaut Press, 1927)

Hadjimichaeli, A. *The Greek Folk Costume* (Vols 1 & 2) (Melissa Publishing, Athens, 1979 and 1984)

Johnstone, Pauline. *A Guide to Greek Island Embroidery* (Victoria and Albert Museum, 1972)
  Turkish Embroidery (Victoria and Albert Museum, 1985)

Kendrick, A. F., Newberry, E. W., and Pesel, L. F. *A Book of Old Embroidery* (Studio, 1921)

Krishna, Mary. 'Zoroastrian Bridal Dress', *Embroidery* (Vol 15 no 4, 1964)

Leix, Alfred. 'Turkestan and its Textile Crafts', *CIBA Review* (Crosby Press, 1974)

Papantoniou, Ioanna. *Greek Costumes* (Peloponnesian Folklore Foundation, 1987)

Pardoe, Julia. *City of the Sultans and Domestic Manners of the Turks in 1836* (Henry Colburn, 1837)

Pesel, Louisa F. *Portfolio No. 2. Stitches from Eastern Embroidery* (Percy Lund, Humphries and Co, 1913)

Ramsay, Mrs. *Everyday Life in Turkey* (Hodder and Stoughton, 1897)

Rolleston, Mary. 'Reminiscences of Mrs Newberry', *Embroidery* (Vol 4 no 2, 1953)

Russell, W. H. *A Diary in the East during the Tour of the Prince and Princess of Wales* (Routledge, 1869)

Scarce, Jennifer. *Women's Costume of the Near and Middle East* (Unwin Hyman, 1987)

Sürür, Ayten. *Türk İşleme Sanati* (1976)

Sykes, Ella. *Persia and its People* (Methuen, 1910)

Trilling, James. *Aegean Crossroads: Greek Island Embroideries in the Textile Museum* (Textile Museum, Washington, 1983)

Valle, Pietro della. *The Journeys of Pietro della Valle* (Folio, 1989)

Wace, Prof. A. J. B. *Mediterranean and Near Eastern Embroideries from the Collection of Mrs F. H. Cook* (Holton and Co, 1935)

Wark, Edna. *Drawn Fabric Embroidery* (Batsford, 1979)

Welters, Linda. *Women's Traditional Costume in Attica* (Peloponnesian Folklore Foundation, 1988)

White, Charles. *Three Years in Constantinople or Domestic Manners of the Turks* (3 vols) (Colburn, 1845)

Zora, P. *Embroidery and Jewellery of Greek National Costumes* (1966)

CHAPTER 4

Elson, Vickie C. *Dowries from Kutch* (University of California, 1979)

Irwin, John, and Hall, Margaret. *Indian Embroideries* (Calico Museum of Textiles, Ahmedabad, 1973)

Marg: A Magazine of Architecture and the Arts (Vol XVII no 2, Embroidery, Bombay, 1964)

Nabholz-Kartashoff, Marie-Louise. *Golden Sprays and Scarlet Flowers. Traditional Indian Textiles from the Museum of Ethnography, Basel, Switzerland* (Shikosha Publishing Co, Japan, 1986)

Paine, Sheila. *Chikan Embroidery* (Shire Publications, 1989)

CHAPTER 5

Snowden, James. *A Bibliography of European Folk Dress* (The Costume Society, 1973)

The Studio (special numbers of the periodical):
  Peasant Art in Sweden, Lapland and Iceland (1910)
  Peasant Art in Austria and Hungary (1911)
  Peasant Art in Russia (1912)
  Peasant Art in Italy (1913)
  Peasant Art in Switzerland (1924)
  Peasant Art in Romania (1929)

CHAPTER 6

Cammann, Schuyler. 'Types of Symbols in Chinese Art' in *Studies in Chinese Thought* (1953)

'Embroidery Techniques in Old China', *Chinese Art Society of America Archives* (Vol XVI no 16, 1962)

Christie, Anthony. *Chinese Mythology* (Newnes, 1968)

Chung, Young Yang. *The Art of Oriental Embroidery* (Scribners, 1979)

Clayre, Alasdair. *The Heart of the Dragon* (Harville and William Collins, 1984)

Hommel, R. P. *China at Work* (Doylestown Bucks County Historical Society, 1921)

Joly, Henri L. *Legends in Japanese Art* (John Lane, The Bodley Head)

Min-hsiung, Shih. *The Silk Industry in Ch'ing (Qing) China* (University of Michigan, 1976)

Staunton, Sir George. *Embassy to China* (1797)

Thompson, John. *China – Its People* (1873)

Vollmer, John. *In the Presence of the Dragon Throne* (Royal Ontario Museum, 1976)

Wilson, Verity. *Chinese Dress* (Victoria and Albert Museum, 1986)

Yarong, Wang. *Chinese Folk Embroidery* (Thames and Hudson, 1987)

ACKNOWLEDGEMENTS

The Embroiderers' Guild wishes to thank the authors and editor for their commitment to this book, Julia Hedgecoe for her superb photography, and Dudley Moss and Peter Williams for kindly donating their photographs.

THE AUTHORS

MEG ANDREWS established the costume and textile department of Sotheby's, Belgravia, in 1980. An expert on Chinese embroidery she now advises collectors, gives lectures – particularly on Chinese Court Costumes – and writes a regular Saleroom column in *Embroidery* magazine.

ELIZABETH BENN (Editor) is a former Chairman of the Embroiderers' Guild and editor of its publication *Embroidery* magazine. For many years she was a staff member and contributor to the *Daily Telegraph*, and now works as a freelance editor and author.

MARIANNE ELLIS has lived and travelled in the Middle East and developed an interest in Turkish embroidery since completing the City and Guilds embroidery course in 1985. Her research has taken her to Turkey, Greece, Canada and the United States, as well as to many museums and collections in the United Kingdom.

ROSEMARY EWLES was the first curator of the Embroiderers' Guild Collection (1981–4), and has held curatorial posts in a number of museums in subjects ranging from agriculture to local history. She is currently Museums Officer at the Museums and Galleries Commission in London.

BARBARA ROWNEY has maintained an interest in Middle-Eastern textiles and artefacts throughout her career in art education, teacher training, further and special education. In 1984 she was granted sabbatical leave to study in Turkey, and since retirement she has been able to travel extensively to continue her research.

LYNN SZYGENDA worked for the Science Museum, and also for the Victoria and Albert Museum in the Department of Textiles, Furnishings and Dress, before being appointed Curator of the Embroiderers' Guild Collection in 1987.

JENNIFER WEARDEN has been a curator in the Department of Textiles, Furnishings and Dress at the Victoria and Albert Museum in London since 1977. She specialises in post-1500 Islamic textiles and in traditional European textiles.

INDEX

INDEX